Knowing
JESUS

 CLASSICS

Knowing
JESUS

JAMES ALISON

 CLASSICS

Society for Promoting Christian Knowledge
36 Causton Street
London SW1P 4ST
www.spckpublishing.co.uk

Copyright © James Alison 1993, 1998
New edition 1998
Reprinted five times
Reissued 2012

British Library Cataloguing-in-Publication Data
A catalogue record for this book is available
from the British Library

ISBN 978-0-281-06503-5

Contents

Foreword

There are some questions in Christian language that look familiar and obvious: everyone is assumed to know what they mean. In this book, James Alison tackles one such question, and does brilliantly what every good teacher should do: he makes the question fresh, unfamiliar, absorbing and challenging. 'Do you have a personal relationship with Jesus?' or, more simply, 'Do you *know* Jesus?' is a question we normally and lazily think we understand. Whatever answers we might give, however relevant or irrelevant we think such a question is, we do not as a rule analyse it that carefully. The result is often a bit of a deadlock. A particular kind of conservative Christian will insist on the necessity of experiencing Jesus as a living individual presence now, like a human friend or neighbour; and a particular kind of liberal Christian will dismiss all this as inappropriate, since our relation to Jesus is a pervasive (but rather elusive) one of being compelled and 'enabled' by his memory.

James Alison's proposals should make both sides of this disagreement think again. No, we do not meet Jesus simply as another human individual; but neither is he just the subject of inspiring stories. We meet Jesus as the *resurrected one* – the one who, after those closest to him have betrayed him and left him to die alone, returns as the source of grace and hope to those treacherous and fearful friends. What this means is that Jesus 'appears' now as the agency of a completely gratuitous love, right outside the calculations, rewards and punishments of human relationships, outside the complicated negotiations for living space that dominate

the 'ordinary' human world, with its underlying
assumption that we all live at each other's expense.
And this makes clear to us as never before just how
deep that assumption goes, and forces us to look afresh
at those at whose expense we live – our victims. The
resurrection of Jesus makes it impossible to take for
granted that the world is nothing but a system of
oppressors and victims, an endless cycle of reactive
violence. We are free to understand ourselves and each
other in a new way, as living in mutual gift not mutual
threat. We can collaborate in the relations that the
resurrection sets in motion, relations of forgiveness,
equality and care. And if we recognize our habitual
bondage to reactive relations, passing on or returning
the wounds we have received, and feel in our lives
together the solid reality of relationships that transcend
this, *then* we 'know Jesus'.

As so often in the context of debates between modern
conservatives and modern liberals, what lifts us out of
a boring and sterile stand-off is a proper rediscovery of
tradition. James Alison is – among other things – re-
stating what some of his Dominican ancestors meant
by 'knowledge through participation', and indeed what
the whole early and medieval Christian tradition
understood as becoming 'divine' in communion with
Christ – growing into freedom, beyond the prison of
self-absorbed, self-referential feelings, beyond the reactive and repetitive world sustained by sin. But this
recovery of older wisdom is given a profoundly
contemporary slant in its concern with violence and
victimage. As a culture, we have become more alert to
the depth and breadth of historical and personal
violence, to just how many victims our 'normative'
culture creates. But if we are to believe in the hope of
something more than just reparation or settling scores,
we need the concrete presence of relations that
transcend reaction, jostling for space, rivalry; we need
Christ and the Church. Here, Alison is deeply influenced

by the theories of René Girard, the French critic and anthropologist, and this book is one of the most attractive and accessible presentations I know of Girard's views.

James Alison's work is a model of clarity in exposition – relaxed, conversational, but holding us firmly to the demands of its subject matter. It is a model of how to deploy some very traditional Christian resources with a thoroughly contemporary intellectual toughness, so as to liberate us from the cliches of so much modern theological squabbling. It is the most imaginative and lucid presentation of a theology of redemption that I have read in many years. But above all, it insists that true theology, truthful reflection on what God is and does, can't be done without conversion to a new perspective on yourself and the world. God is not to be known unless we grasp the depth of our freedom and our unfreedom, unless we give up fictions about our purity or our innocence and become committed to searching out those we exclude and suppress, creating with them the promised community of mutual gift. This is the community that depends on the resurrection of Jesus; to belong wholeheartedly to it is to know Jesus – and the God whom Jesus called 'Father'.

Rowan Williams

Introduction

A preacher, it is said, is the last one to hear his own sermon. Certainly that has been true for me. Since *Knowing Jesus* came out in 1993, I have found myself continually challenged by things which I wrote far too easily – things which led me into dangerous waters in the countries in which I was working. I found that I had to learn an awful lot, especially about being loved, and finding myself painfully set free from acting out of violent and resentful patterns of desire. One of the pleasures of this process has been the response of people who clearly understood what I had been saying much more clearly and fully than I did myself, people who found that *Knowing Jesus* opened up for them newer and better ways of becoming Church.

It thus seemed particularly appropriate, when Joanna Moriarty of SPCK and I discussed a possible reprint, that a new edition should appear with questions which made the book more user-friendly for Lenten discussion groups. It is one thing to understand something new of the Gospel in quiet and meditative reading. It is another to find oneself opened up by hearing how others see the same questions, and to discover different ways in which the same questions can challenge us.

I have therefore included some questions at the end of each chapter, which are designed to enable groups to undergo a richer Lenten journey. My hope is that by group meditation on these questions, we will come to a more powerful experience of living Easter in our daily lives, and a fuller sense of how ordinary participation in liturgy, and particularly the Eucharist, can fire us up to imagine new and daring forms of creating fraternity.

My thanks to Brendan Walsh, my original editor at SPCK, whose initial bet in taking on *Knowing Jesus* has been of such value to me personally, to Joanna Moriarty whose dedication has navigated the paths of making this new edition possible, but above all to those readers of the book and practitioners of the Christian faith whose response and comeback has been so generous and stimulating.

James Alison
London, August 1998

1
The Resurrection

Let's start with a quote from someone else:

What is the primary aim of all evangelization and of all catechesis? Possibly that of teaching people a certain number of eternal truths, or of passing on Christian values to the rising generation? No, it is to bring people to a personal encounter with Jesus Christ the only Saviour by making them his 'disciples'.

Perhaps this was said by Billy Graham, or the new Archbishop of Canterbury? No, it was part of an advent retreat given to the papal household in 1989 by a Capuchin professor of theology, Raniero Cantalamessa (see *Jesus Christ, the Holy One of God*, St Paul Publications, p. 89). This is not some special language reserved to Protestants, or charismatics. It appears right in the centre of the Church.

You may have come across this sort of language before. I mean language of the sort, 'Do you know Jesus?' or, 'Do you have a personal relationship with Jesus Christ?' Now, there are many possible answers to those questions. Some readers may be able to answer, unambiguously, and without any feeling of being forced: 'Yes, I do know Jesus' or, 'Yes, I do have a personal relationship with Jesus Christ.' In which case, I may not have much to offer you in this book, or, perhaps, what I do offer may help you increase and develop that knowledge, that relationship. Maybe, on the other hand, you do not want to answer those sort of questions; you feel that you don't know what the questions mean, or else you feel bullied by them, as though they were forcing you to take a stand, so that if you don't answer, or answer in the negative, you feel like St Peter standing in the courtyard and saying, 'I tell you, I don't know him'.

Except of course, that you might well not be in a position to do anything so grand as to make some sort of betrayal of your faith. You just feel that someone is using a phrase, a way of talking, to make you feel inferior, to suggest to you that you aren't really 'in' on the centre of the Christian faith.

Well, what I hope to be doing in this book is to try and look at a way of talking that can now be found at the very centre of the Church, and talk of an experience, or set of experiences, which are thought to be at the very centre of what it means to be a Christian at the end of the twentieth century.

The standard way of beginning to look at the question of knowing Jesus might well be to take the object, and see what we can know about Jesus, and then take the subject, and see what we can discover about how we know anybody, with a view to aligning our 'knowing selves' to the object we find out about. I don't think that would be very useful. It would already be accepting an understanding of what it is to know a person, and what of a person we can know, that I consider unhelpful. Ultimately, it lands us with a picture of the other as radically unknown to us, radically foreign, and of ourselves as lonely little knowers striving in vain for a knowledge that we fear we can never really attain.

To be sure, for convenience's sake, I'll sometimes appear to divide the world between subject and object. However, if I really am stuck in that, then I won't have communicated what I want to about knowing Jesus. The way we can avoid being caught in the trap of whether knowledge is objective or subjective is by looking at the category of 'witness', for that is how we know anything at all about Jesus: our access to him is the apostolic witness.

During the last twenty years, tens of thousands,

perhaps hundreds of thousands, of Guatemalan Indians have been murdered. It is highly likely that among them was at least one thirty-three-year-old man. Yet, we hear of no growing movement to proclaim that Francisco, let us say, is God. Nor do we hear of many people who claim to have a personal relationship with Francisco. What is it that has made it possible for people to talk about Jesus in a quite different way from our talking about Francisco?

The answer, as you know, is the resurrection. It is the resurrection that makes it possible for this conversation to be happening at all. Let's explore what we can of the resurrection, and see what it means. Some people talk of the resurrection as though it were a simple proof that Jesus was what he said he was, and that's an end to it. However, I'd like to suggest that the beginning and end of any question to do with knowing Jesus lies in enriching our understanding of the resurrection.

Let us remember certain basic facts. We have a faith at all because we receive a witness. That is to say, starting from a Sunday morning in the first century, a group of people began to make extraordinary claims about someone who had been killed the Friday before. Something had happened to him, and something had clearly happened to them. Over a period of twenty or thirty years or more, these people both bore witness to what they had experienced, and began to develop their understanding of it, setting it down in writing, with the help of others. Because of what they had experienced, they were able to work through their memories, and understand even better their relationship to, and the experiences they had shared with, the man who had been killed. They were able to start to make a unified sense out of what they hadn't properly understood beforehand in the teaching and actions of the man who had been killed.

This is traditionally called the apostolic witness: the witness of the apostles to Jesus. It was a witness that

could have had no sense at all had the one killed
remained simply dead, like Francisco in Guatemala.
What the apostles witness to is the resurrection, the
irruption of a happening into their lives and one that
could be experienced in a variety of ways. It was not
simply a fact that they could then tack on to the end of
the creed, so that it would be a fuller account of what
had happened. It was what made it possible for there to
be a creed at all. If there had been no resurrection, there
would have been no New Testament, since the New
Testament *is* the witness of the apostles to the
resurrection, including their new-found ability to understand what led to it. Without it, there would have been
no new story to tell.

What we have, then, is a witness. We receive this
witness in the community which receives the teaching
of the apostles. We receive the New Testament, and we
also receive the Old Testament, as an aid to understanding what the New Testament is about. Indeed, we can't
understand what Jesus was doing, or what the
resurrection meant, and means, without seeing what it
was that formed him, in what context he gave his
teaching and lived his life. All that means receiving the
Old Testament. The witness of the apostles that we
have received is a witness which includes the Old
Testament so that they, the apostles, can explain to us,
what was the full meaning of the happening on that
Sunday morning after Jesus had been killed. I hope
that that will become clearer during the course of this
book.

I stress all this, because some people treat the
gospels, for instance, as if they were biographies of
Jesus, sort of primitive history books. They are nothing
of the sort. They are witnesses to the apostolic
experience of the resurrection, and the rewriting of their
experience of the last years before the resurrection in its
light. Some people treat the Old Testament as though it
were a manual of laws and practices. Again, that won't

do. We receive the Old Testament because it reveals the pattern of God's dealings with his chosen people, dealings which give models for understanding what God really wanted to reveal when he raised Jesus from the dead.

So, the first point which I'd like to establish before we can get anywhere near talking about how we may know Jesus, is that the only access we have to Jesus, the only reason that Jesus isn't to us like a dead Guatemalan Indian, is that we receive witnesses to his resurrection. That is what the New Testament is: the apostolic witness set down in writing, which is the norm of the faith of the Church.

Now, please note, that witness is not merely a witness to the fact of the resurrection, though it certainly is that. It is not merely saying: yes, we can affirm that on such and such a day, the dead man Jesus of Nazareth did in fact rise from the dead. They *are* saying that. Paul says that in 1 Corinthians 15.3-8: 'I handed on to you . . . that he was raised on the third day in accordance with the scriptures, and that he appeared to Cephas . . .' But even more than bearing witness to an event, as you or I might witness a traffic accident, they are witnesses *from* the resurrection. That is to say, it was a happening which profoundly changed them, not only turning pusillanimous fisherfolk into international heroes and martyrs, but causing them to rethink the whole of their lives, their relationship with their homeland, their culture, its values, and radically altering their understanding of who God is.

You see, already, the gap between subjective and objective has disappeared. What happened 'out there' – Jesus' appearances to the apostles, and what happened 'in here' – the transformation that this produced, are part of the same phenomenon: the presence of the risen Lord. They are not only witnesses of, but witnesses from. Furthermore, it is clear that there is no such thing as just a witness *of* the resurrection. It was not the sort of happening that could be witnessed casually, as I witness a rattlesnake shedding its skin, while riding by smoking my Marlboro'. The very fact of witnessing it at all meant a degree of involvement in a complex set of human relationships, which culminated in their being able to witness it. That was true of all the disciples to whom Jesus appeared. Jesus' appearances to them took place within the framework of their friendship with him, their hopes concerning him, their disillusionment concerning him, their feeling of guilt at having abandoned him. Even Saul did not become a witness out of a clear sky: he became a witness precisely as his involvement in persecuting the witnesses was turned on its head. He saw the risen one simultaneously as he saw that he had been persecuting God. Because the risen one is God as persecuted – but we'll be looking at that later on.

Let me fill that out a bit more fully. In all of the gospels Jesus, who is clearly a figure of considerable charisma, attracts a following with whom he plays hard-to-get. He wants people to follow him, but not on their terms. He subverts their understanding of what he is doing, and indeed of what they are doing following him. He won't allow them to see him as the expected Messiah in any straightforward way; while he is happy with the category of 'prophet' he clearly goes beyond it, showing a power and an authority beyond Moses, and Elijah, and Joshua, and other prophets. He always emphasizes the way in which the prophets' paths led them to a violent death. So, the relationship between Jesus and his followers is shown in all the gospels to be a highly complex one, leading them on, but constantly sifting their intentions, their motives, their understanding of what they're about.

At the same time, he clearly indicates what they could only understand afterwards, that he is going to be killed, and that they would abandon him. For all of them, their relationship to him ends in a tragedy. Let me emphasize that again. On Good Friday, the disciples' relationship with Jesus ended. Because Jesus died. The relationship ended in just the same way as my relationship with my aunt Barley ended when she died. The set of feelings, the memories, the elations and frustrations shared with, or caused by Barley, didn't end. They remain to be worked through by me. But the relationship ended because it was no longer mutual. So, the disciples had all those loose ends, of curiosity, of doubt, of commitment, of memory, but suddenly they had them in a vacuum.

It was not merely a neutral vacuum, as when someone loved or admired dies far away from where you are and without any possibility of your having done something to prevent it. It was a tragic vacuum, because one of the feelings informing it was guilt at having abandoned Jesus, a sense of moral failure. It is easy enough for us to look at St Peter as the 'goody' who cried after the cock crowed, and Judas as the 'baddy', who hanged himself when he realised what he'd done. But that picture hides an important similarity between them, and obscures the real tragedy of Judas' death. Both betrayed Jesus, along with all the others who ran away; the difference was between the type of betrayal that involves letting down your cause at a crucial point, and the type that involves active collaboration with the other side. However, Judas' terminal sin was not his treachery (with all due respect to Dante), but his inability to believe in the possibility of forgiveness – what we usually call despair.

Do you remember the few days in August 1991 when there was an attempted coup in the former Soviet Union? I remember it well enough (and this was written on the day that the coup ended) to recall that even when the news of the coup first broke, a number of people, myself included, thought and hoped and prayed that the people would not let it happen, and that it would be reversed. That is to say, when the coup was announced, there was implicit in that kind of historical event, at least the possibility of its undoing. So, for sixty hours, we could hope and pray and watch TV, and detect signs of the coup's collapse. Our relationship with Gorbachev's government was not abruptly, and for ever, severed, as it would have been had Gorbachev been shot. That is quite different from the experience of the disciples. Their relationship with Jesus *was* for ever, and abruptly, severed. They had no hope of waiting to see if Jesus would come back from the Crimea. Death was not like the Crimea. There were no signs that something might change, that God might revoke death. There was just a termination; they were left like live cables off which a computer has been yanked and burned, leaving them powerless to receive or transmit information.

That of course led to the beginnings of mourning. Probably not immediate mourning, for the shock of Jesus' arrest, death, and the disciples' disbanding, was probably too great for immediate mourning. Luke gives us some idea of the early desolation of the disciples who were walking to Emmaus. And all of this took place within an atmosphere of fear. You remember that the disciples met on Easter evening behind locked doors. This was not because news of the resurrection had leaked out, and they were frightened of people protesting at the new religion that was starting up, as people might sometimes think. It was because they were foreigners in the capital of a police state. They had had to face two distinct lots of military figures, Jewish and Roman, and they were, by their accents, and probably their dress, suspect of involvement with a major criminal, who had been done away with amidst tumultuous scenes. At the time, let us remember, they probably thought of themselves as to some degree part of a politico-messianic movement. Their understanding of what they were about was not yet that of Jesus – witness their question to him even after the resurrection, and just before the ascension: 'Lord, is this the time when you will restore the kingdom of Israel?' (Acts 1.6). All of that will have caused them to feel the danger of their own situation maybe rather more acutely than they need have. However, that fear was a dominant factor in their lives at that point need not be doubted.

Now, please notice what I'm not doing here. I'm *not* trying to fill in a sort of historical romance, you know the sort of thing: 'what Mary Queen of Scots' maid thought as her mistress was led to the block at Fotheringay'. I'm not trying to give an imaginary psychological description of the disciples. I'm trying rather to bring out the ordinary human responses to Jesus' death that were present. That is to say, whose absence would have been remarkable, and the sign of deeply psychologically deranged personalities. These responses are either present or hinted at in the New Testament texts. The reason for this is to illustrate something of the network of relationships into which Jesus began to appear, starting on that Sunday morning. The resurrection was first perceived from within those complexes of relationships that had been left severed and dangling on the Friday before, and had been developed over the years leading up to that.

The very earliest strata of the New Testament witness tell us a number of things about the resurrection - not film-set details, but rather more than that. They tell us, for instance, that the resurrection was in the first place something that happened to Jesus. It seems odd to say so, but many people have a lingering feeling that perhaps the resurrection was a set of experiences in the lives of the disciples, worked, maybe, by God, but in the absence of Jesus, who was not in his tomb, but wasn't anywhere else either. That view simply will not bear the evidence of the texts. Paul, in the first letter to the Thessalonians, probably the earliest of the New Testament texts to be written, tells us of 'God's Son from heaven, whom he raised from the dead - Jesus'

(1.10). It could not be clearer in Peter's first speech to Jerusalem in Acts: 'This Jesus God raised up, and of that all of us are witnesses' (2.32).

This is clear from the way in which some of the texts refer to Jesus' resurrection as his vindication (1 Tim. 3.16) over against his enemies. That is to say, one of the first understandings of the resurrection was that it was God showing that Jesus was right, and his enemies were wrong. This is only hinted at; soon the disciples' understanding seems to have deepened into seeing that this was too colossal an event merely to be seen as God settling scores with a number of executioners. But there is enough of this sentiment present to show that the disciples definitely did see themselves as, if you like, onlookers at a prize fight, in which their champion was vindicated, a perception that cannot be explained by a subjective explosion of feeling about Jesus having been raised by God.

First, the resurrection was seen as something that happened to Jesus, the making full of what it meant to be Lord and Messiah (Acts 2.36) that he had lived up to and into his death. Then, second, it revealed something about God. For, in raising Jesus from the dead, God confirmed the life and death of Jesus, affirmed the freedom and truth of Jesus' life. God gave himself to be defined as the God who raised Jesus from the dead, a new and completely unexpected and radical new insight into who God is. Third, the resurrection began to transform the lives of the disciples; they began to be able to understand anew the life and death of Jesus, and the way in which the Scriptures pointed to what they had witnessed. They began to be able to rewrite their lives from an entirely unexpected new vantage point.

Now, what was it that made the resurrection have such density? I don't mean, what did it look like, or even, what did it feel like. What I mean is: how did the resurrection irrupt into that network of tangled, sorry relationships that were jarring painfully by Easter Saturday? Of what, insofar as we can describe a unique and a normative experience, was the resurrection experience made up? There are hints in the New Testament, but these are difficult to identify because of the familiarity of the texts, and because we know what is coming next. I would suggest that the first category by which we can look at this is that of *gratuity*.

It is almost impossible to imagine the shock of the sheer gratuity of the resurrection. Gratuity is when someone gives something to us without any interest attached at all, when we are moved by something that is quite outside the network of relationships, friendships, economic and political ties that constitute our life. It is when something appears in our life that has no reference at all to what we feel we need, or deserve, and over which we have no control, no ability to manipulate. Occasionally, we do experience hints of something like this, but mostly all of us are tied in to the rhythms of the expected, the reciprocated, the demanded, the earned, or the punished.

Now, the resurrection was entirely gratuitous. It was gratuitous for Jesus, an act of love by the Father, not a payment for deserving service. Where it is suggested in Hebrews 5.7-9 that Jesus deserved the resurrection for us, this has nothing to do with Jesus having acquired a right over against the Father, a debt which the Father had to honour. What is being talked about there is an exchange of love - the love lived out in obedience in Jesus' life, a love made possible by Jesus' being loved in the first place. In no exchange of love are words like 'deserving' or 'earning' other than weak metaphors - at least from the viewpoint of the participants: their mutual self-giving is gratuitous, and urges no rights.

If then the resurrection was gratuitous for Jesus, it must have seemed even more so for the disciples. It was quite outside their experience, and indeed, in the form it took, quite outside the possibility of human vocabulary. Nothing in popular Jewish belief in a resurrection on the last day had led them to prepare for this. It had nothing at all to do with any system, or structure, or order, or network, or relationship to which any of them belonged. It was for them something utterly 'other'. To say that it was surprising, unprecedented, and so on, is not enough. The gratuity of the resurrection, and its utter otherness, were part of the same package – the life of Jesus – that so disconcerted the disciples. If there's anything clear from the accounts of the appearances it's exactly this element of consternation, fear, the inability to recognize at first. The way Jesus had to preface his remarks with 'Peace, be not afraid' points to this.

Let's look at this: for the irruption of what is utterly other, utterly gratuitous, is not simply a delightful thing. It is a terrifying one. Whilst we may feel hemmed in by, and in conflict with, what I call the 'customary' other, the set of relationships in which we have been formed, and within which we normally move, both personal, historical, economic, political, at the same time these relationships do at least give us a certain security. What is other to us, in a more distant sense, if you like, the 'removed' other, like visiting a foreign country whose language we don't know, and whose culture we don't understand, is both exciting and frightening. It is exhilarating as we see new things, and learn about new possibilities, and are able to relativize our own ways of doing things, but it is also frightening, in that we are vulnerable to being moved by the other in ways which we aren't at home. Things like police and soldiers seem less dependable, not because they are, but because we don't know what to expect, and wouldn't know how to cope if we were to get into trouble. We sense that we might be much more easily victimized if things went wrong, we'd have less chance in a foreign court of law.

Well, if that's true of the 'removed' other where we do have a certain sense of shared basic human sensitivity with the locals, then how much truer is it of the 'utterly' other, the purely gratuitous that in its first manifestation it is both exhilarating and terrifying. However, the risen Lord was not only utterly 'other', for it was possible for the disciples to recognize him. After a bit they were able to say, 'It is the Lord'. However, this was not a case of encountering something familiar in the midst of what was other. It was not as if, lost in the middle of Tibet, you suddenly came across someone who offered you tea and biscuits like in England. That would be to suggest that Jesus had somehow 'passed over', and was a bit of who he had been now stuck in the other world: we would be in the realm of ghosts, and spirit divination. No, what the disciples were able to experience was that the wholly, gratuitously other, was made present to them as a giving back of someone familiar. Not someone from this side gone there, but someone from there given in a wholly new way, that was yet a continuation of the way they had sensed him as being given while he was with them before his death. This meant that the wholly, gratuitously, utterly other was no longer simply strange, but, without ceasing to be other, was a presence of recognizable, familiar, love for them. This was the beginning of the recasting of the disciples' perception of God, the wholly 'other', in terms of Jesus, the risen Lord.

Everything else said about the resurrection must be a way of qualifying this irruption of the utterly gratuitous other. In the first place, this utterly gratuitous other is the giving back of a freely loving person, it is not a ghost. A ghost haunts, it plays on memories, it is a sign of condemnation, it must be got rid of if we are to live in peace. Do you remember Herod's feeling of guilt when he thought that Jesus was John the Baptist risen from the dead (Mark 6.14–16)? For him, the presence was not gratuitous, it was an accusation from within the world of his own actions, a vengeance from beyond the tomb. No, the risen Jesus was not haunting, which would not be gratuitous, he was communicating, purely gratuitously, as a person.

Furthermore, the irruption of the gratuitous 'other' happened within the disciples' frame of reference. They were frightened, ashamed, muddled, disappointed; the irruption didn't depend on them being in the 'right' mood. And it happened as *forgiveness*. This is the second great category of the experience of the resurrection. Part of the utterly gratuitous other is that it is entirely outside any system of retribution and desert, and is therefore experienced by us as loosing us from being tied in to the 'customary' other. The gratuitous other quite undermines all things that do not depend on gratuity, both our wounded relationships, and our virtues, which involve elements of protection and security. It is both as forgiveness of our sins and complete restructuring of our virtues that the gratuitous other reaches us.

The resurrection is forgiveness: not a decree of forgiveness, but the presence of gratuity as a person. The simple fact of Jesus' appearance to his disciples, as soon as they had recovered from their consternation at the presence of what was quite outside their experience, was the presence of forgiveness. Their sorrow, and guilt, and confusion, could be loosed within them, because the focus of their sorrow and guilt and confusion had come back from right outside it, and was not affected by it. There was no element in the presence of the risen Jesus of any reciprocating by Jesus of what had been done to him. If there had been his presence would not have been outside our human tit-for-tat, it would not have been gratuitous, and it would not have been forgiving.

So, Jesus tells his disciples in John (20.23):'Receive the Holy Spirit. If you forgive the sins of any, they are forgiven them; if you retain any, they are retained', and in Luke (24.47), that 'repentance and forgiveness of sins' is to be preached in his name to all nations. It is the presence of the gratuitous other as forgiveness that is given in the Holy Spirit, and it is this that is to be made available to all nations. The gratuitous other has irrupted into the network and construction of human relationships as forgiveness. The resurrection can never be approached without these categories.

The third category with which the resurrection may be described is that of sending, or *mission*. The utterly other, gratuitously present as forgiveness, doesn't just irrupt into the lives of the disciples. It sends them to the ends of the earth. Inseparable from the gratuity and the forgiveness is the communication. It is a communication that is from the other, not part of any communication we know, or can construct. It is given so as to be given, expanding gratuitously. It is not even a motive for doing something, in the ordinary sense of the word. I may be sent to Thailand to sell security paper for making banknotes. I have a motive for going. However, to be sent to Thailand to preach repentance and forgiveness of sins is not on the same level. One is a motive within the structure of motives and actions and debts that keeps the world ticking over. The other is quite gratuitous, and dependent on no structure from the world at all. It shares in the gratuity of what is utterly other.

So far, I have been trying to open out the mystery of the resurrection in such a way as to make it the centre from which any talk of knowing Jesus, or having a personal relationship with him, flows. Now I shall be suggesting that it is not only the centre, but also the criterion for any such knowledge, and any such relationship.

In looking at the resurrection, and how it burst in on

the disciples, turning them into apostles, there are three interlinked categories by which we can begin to approximate to the disciples' experience of the resurrection: gratuity, forgiveness, and mission. This is by no means all that we can derive from the New Testament with regards to the presence of the risen Lord, though without these elements to help us structure our understanding, I think we would be unfaithful to the witness.

What I want to examine now are two more, rather curious, and again interlinked, aspects of the resurrection that fill out even further the witness to the risen Lord. John's gospel is insistent that the risen Jesus had the marks of the nails in his hands and feet. Luke's gospel at least hints as much by having Jesus certify his identity by showing his hands and his feet: it is the presence of the marks of his death that shows that he is the same man, just as it is the physical nature of his presence that shows that he is not a ghost. Jesus' identity is revealed by the evidence of his death.

Link that to the key story of the first resurrection appearance in Luke, which is to the disciples on the road to Emmaus, and we are able to start filling out our picture. There we have the sense of mystery, the otherness of Jesus, only recognized late on; but more important, Jesus is recognized at the climax of the explanation he gives to the disciples of the true meaning of the Scriptures. The key to that explanation is that the Messiah must suffer and die before entering into his glory, and the climax is the shared meal to which that explanation led. Jesus' presence, and the illumination of what his death was about, are part of the same experience for the disciples at Emmaus. It is surely one of the most difficult points to explain in our faith, that Jesus appeared as the risen Lord, but not only as the risen Lord. He appeared as the crucified-and-risen Lord. Jesus' appearance to the disciples at Emmaus involved the making present of the necessary death as part of the risen density of his presence.

Let me try to say what I mean, or rather, what I think the apostolic witness means. If we talk about Jesus as risen Lord, we often imagine a picture of dying and rising again that is perhaps rather like going to bed and getting up again, or planting a seed, and waiting for it to burst forth afterwards. Now, although there are hints of this way of talking in the parables, I'd like to challenge it as a way of understanding our Lord's resurrection. This picture has two elements which I regard as unhelpful in dealing with the resurrection witness. The first is a sense of chronological continuity. First there was the death, then there was the resurrection; just as, first she went to bed, then she got up. It would be nonsense to say that the lady making coffee was the sleeping-and-awakened one, unless you meant that she was neither really asleep, nor really awake, just half-dazed. No, in the sleeping/awaking model, first she was asleep, then she was awake.

Well, I want to suggest that this is not a proper analogy for the resurrection. The resurrection was, *for the disciples*, the next step in the story: for them, first Jesus was dead, then he was alive. But *it was not so for Jesus*. For Jesus, the resurrection was the giving back of the whole of his human life, leading up to, and including his death. It was not simply the next stage in his human life. To illustrate my point, let us suppose that Jesus' birthday had been on Easter Saturday. He was thirty-three when he was killed on Good Friday. But he was not thirty-four when he rose on Easter Sunday. He was not any age at all. He was his whole human life and death given back by God.

The second element of the sleeping and rising model that I find unhelpful is the way in which the second state – rising, or giving forth fruit, is contained implicitly in the first, going to sleep, or planting a seed in the earth. This is what one might call the chrysalis model of the resurrection. Jesus lived his earthly life as a caterpillar, then went into a chrysalis, and at the resurrection emerged as the beautiful butterfly which we all know and love. Now again, this is unhelpful because it suggests that the power behind the change was within the changed one, just as the butterfly is implicit in the caterpillar. Whereas the point of Jesus' resurrection was that there was no power at all within the dead Jesus. The power to raise him was purely from the Father, not a hidden resource in some remote corner of Jesus that hadn't been reached by death. The raising of Jesus was not, if you like, a logical continuation of the life and power that had been in Jesus before. Rather, the raising of Jesus was the gratuitous giving back of the whole life and death that had ended on Good Friday – the whole of Jesus' humanity includes his human death.

Now what that means is that the risen Lord is simultaneously the dead-and-risen Lord. Jesus as he appeared to the disciples was not, as it were, the champion who has showered down after the match; he appeared on a completely different level. If there's any phrase that comes near expressing this, it is 'the living dead'. Not, obviously, in the Hollywood sense of someone caught in a time warp between being dead and going to an eternal rest, whether up or down, but in the sense that the resurrection life was the giving back of the whole human life, leading up to and including the death. It is this that is the sign that death has been conquered, that the resurrection life isn't on the same level as death, just cancelling it out, as it were. The resurrection life includes the human death of Jesus. He is always present after the resurrection simultaneously as crucified and as risen Lord.

Just in case you think I'm making this up, may I refer you to the Easter Preface number III in the Roman Missal. There we are told that Jesus is 'still our priest, our advocate who always pleads our cause. Christ is the victim who dies no more, the Lamb once slain who lives for ever'. What the Latin of the Preface in fact says is, 'agnus qui vivit semper occisus', which literally means 'who lives forever slain' – closer to the idea of the living dead than the English translation. The same idea comes up in all those hymns in the book of Revelation, where the seer sees Jesus as 'a Lamb standing as if it had been slaughtered' (Rev. 5.6). This is well captured in certain medieval pictures, such as Van Eyck's 'Adoration of the Lamb', or Grünewald's Isenheim Altarpiece. The artists represent the living Lamb, standing with a banner, or an empty cross, to symbolize the resurrection. Out of the Lamb's slaughtered neck blood flows into a chalice. That is about as good an image of the simultaneously crucified and risen Lord as we can manage. It is the slaughtered one who is made alive, given back in the resurrection. It is not as though the resurrection cured him of being slaughtered – (he was in a bad way but God bandaged him up) – the gratuity of the resurrection is what gives him back as the slaughtered one. It is here that the devotion to Christ crucified has its place in the lives of some of the saints. It is here that stigmatists like St Francis or Padre Pio bear witness to the life of the risen Lord. The mistake is when people oppose the crucified Lord to the risen Lord, imagining perhaps that 'a true spiritual life requires a balance between these two'. There is no opposition, for the presence of the crucified Lord is within the presence of the risen Lord. It is as crucified Lord that Jesus is risen. As we will see, the presence of Jesus as risen-slaughtered one is key to the sense in which the resurrection is the presence of forgiveness, is the forgiveness of sins.

The last of the resurrection appearances to a person, making of that person an apostle, an authentic witness to the resurrection, was the rather strange, *sui generis*, appearance to Paul. Strange and *sui generis* because

Paul had had, as far as we know, no contact with Jesus of Nazareth before his death. That is, he had no personal historical recollection of the life of Jesus, or his teaching, to be deepened, transformed and authenticated by the appearance of the risen Lord. Paul's relationship to Jesus was simply that of trying to wipe out, out of zeal for the Lord of hosts, the false 'Way' that was spreading in the wake of Jesus' death. Saul, as he then was, would have been convinced that when it came to persecuting, it mattered entirely whose side you were on. It would be, for instance, wicked to be part of a foreign persecution of, say, the Maccabees, because that was to persecute God's own faithful ones. On the other hand, it was certainly right to persecute, in the name of the Lord, those who were undermining the true faith in the God of Moses.

Jesus appeared to Paul on the road to Damascus as the persecuted one. 'Who are you, Lord?' 'I am Jesus, whom you are persecuting' (Acts 9.5). That was the impact of the risen Lord on Paul – not the triumphant one, the victorious one, but the persecuted one. The dynamic is the same as I have been describing with relation to the appearances to the disciples in John and Luke. The risen Lord is the persecuted-and-risen Lord. Or rather, the impact made on Paul is that when he perceives that it is God whom he has been persecuting, in the name of God, it is the presence of God as persecuted that is, to him, forgiveness; that is to him the possibility of an entirely new life, a radical re-ordering of everything he had believed. The gratuitous presence was that of the crucified one. Not as accusation, but as forgiveness. Because of the persecution in which he was involved, Paul was able to perceive his involvement in the persecution of God, and was thus able to receive a huge change of life, a change by which he came to worship God as victim: to preach Christ crucified, and to know only Christ, and him crucified. Again, the risen Lord has risen as the crucified one.

Now that, the simultaneous presence of the risen life in the crucified one, is what is called a mystery. Please notice that a 'mystery' is not here something obscurantist, or intellectually dubious, as when someone runs out of logical things to say, and retreats into talking piffle as a cover-up. I think I'm saying something that is making reasonable use of categories we possess, but to indicate something of a density that is not part of our normal experience. I'm saying that the risen Jesus is risen as simultaneously crucified to death, and living, both of which are categories we can understand separately, but which it would never normally occur to us to imagine together. It is not merely a question of simultaneity, as if I were claiming that two mutually exclusive states were simultaneously present – some sort of paradox, like a room which is simultaneously noisy and silent. I am saying that the resurrection was the giving back of the life and the death at the same time. If you like, the resurrection life is not on the same level as ordinary life, which is annihilated at death, rather it is able to include both the life and the death which concludes it, precisely because it is the free giving and giving back of both. Once again, it is the element of pure gratuity in the giving and giving back which is what is not on the same level as life or death, and is thus able to make both present simultaneously.

I ask your patience if this appears to be bizarre. It is, I would suggest, the experience that is at the centre of the Christian faith, from which starting point the other pivotal doctrines – of the Incarnation and the Trinity – were discovered. The density of the presence to the apostles of the risen Jesus lay in the fact that he was risen as the crucified one. Much of the rest of this book will be an attempt to unpack the density of this presence.

There is however one further, and final, aspect of the

presence of the risen Lord that by its very obviousness can easily be overlooked, or ignored. That is that the risen Lord is human. Often we are so concerned with such questions as: what sort of body did Jesus have, was the resurrection physical, and so on, that we fail to notice what is perhaps the really important thing of which the physical appearances of Jesus were signs. That is, that the crucified and risen Jesus was not only crucified as a human, but rose as a crucified human.

It is I think important to hold on to this, since there is a tendency, helped by the apparent vagueness of the gospel texts when they deal with the resurrection, to imagine that Jesus may well have been human up until his death, but from the resurrection onwards, he reverted to being God, and eventually, like a helium balloon, couldn't be held to the earth any longer, and floated back to heaven where he belonged.

Well, this is not the case. When Jesus died, it was a fully human being who died completely, and when Jesus was raised from the dead, it was a human being who was given back to us. Given back as a crucified and living human being. I stress this for two reasons: first, and incidentally, because if we don't hold on to this, we make a nonsense of the belief in the ascension. The special form of the Eucharistic prayer for the Mass of the Ascension says:

> In union with the whole Church we celebrate that day when your only Son our Lord took his place with you and raised our frail human nature to glory.

That is to say, the ascension was not Jesus beaming back up to Starship Enterprise when the Mission was accomplished, leaving the earthlings to play happily; it was the introduction of a novelty into heaven: human nature. Being human was from then on permanently and indissolubly involved in the presence of God.

However, the issue of the ascension is, for my purpose here, an aside. What is important is that the risen and crucified Jesus was no less human after his resurrection than before it. This not only says something about the presence of human nature in heaven, but something about the presence of God on earth. The divine life is indissolubly and permanently present as human. All divine dealings with humanity are on a human level.

Now, this may sound like some sort of clever exercise in logic. It is nothing of the sort: I think rather that it's this sort of insistence which helps us to relativize a whole lot of pious thinking. It means that being religious, or knowing Jesus, can have nothing to do with fleeing upwards, with escaping from being human, avoiding being flesh and blood, being moved by bodies and emotions. That the Church understands sacraments to be the ordinary means by which divine life is available to humans illustrates this, for sacraments are all to do with the physical celebrations by which divine life penetrates our human histories.

I insist on this now, not primarily for its own sake, but because unless we understand that, two things become really quite incomprehensible. If Jesus had not risen as a human being, he could have floated about indefinitely, appearing and disappearing. Yet the apostolic witness clearly makes a distinction between Jesus, and the Holy Spirit. Jesus had to go because he was a particular human being, not a general ghostly presence. It was his going that made possible the coming of the Holy Spirit, not because the Holy Spirit is a general ghostly presence, but because the Holy Spirit is not a particular human being. It is important to understand however, that while the Holy Spirit is not a particular human being, what it makes present to the apostles is made present on an entirely human level.

Again, this is not an easy point to make, so let me recap what I have been trying to do. I have been trying to fill out the density of the presence of the risen Lord to the apostles, so as to give some possibility of our entering into the experience which they had, to which they bear witness, and which is normative for any experience of Jesus which we might have. At a certain point after the resurrection the apostles ceased to receive experiences of the particular human being Jesus of Nazareth, and started to receive a slightly different experience which had to do with, but was not the same as, their previous experience of Jesus. I'd like to explore that a little.

So, what *was* the difference between the way Jesus was present to the apostles in his resurrection appearances, and his presence thereafter? Well, I've underlined two ways of Jesus' being present to them: his actual physical presence, by which he appeared, they could touch him, and he could eat fish; and, along with that, and as part of it, the gratuitous forgiving presence that called them out of themselves towards the other whom they found difficult to recognize, and which gradually transformed their lives. These two came together in the case of the apostles. They do not come together for us. The physical appearances of Jesus came to an end after an interval which Luke puts at the symbolic figure of forty days, though the surprise appearance to Saul was later. During that period, Jesus taught them about the kingdom of God (Acts 1.3), and helped the fulness of the novelty of the resurrection sink in. Then he ascended to heaven, and shortly thereafter, the Holy Spirit came upon the apostles.

That's how Luke presents it. John's approach is rather different. He has Jesus breathe the Holy Spirit into the apostles on the first evening of the resurrection. Then Jesus carries on appearing for a time, but there is no Pentecost in John. Jesus breathes the Spirit saying, 'Receive the Holy Spirit. If you forgive the sins of any, they are forgiven; if you retain the sins of any, they are retained' (John 20.22).

In Luke the Father sends the Holy Spirit from on high, and in John, Jesus breathes the Holy Spirit, but in both cases the Holy Spirit is the Spirit of the risen

Lord, the Spirit that was in Christ. The Spirit constantly makes present the crucified and risen Lord, thus perpetually reproducing those changes of relationship which the risen Lord had started to produce as a result of his resurrection. What I'm trying to say is that outside the group of apostles who were physical witnesses to the resurrected Lord, no one gets to see the physically risen Lord. But instead, all the really important elements of the resurrection – the irruption into our lives of gratuity as forgiveness, permitting a recasting of relationships – all that, is made constantly available to us by the Holy Spirit, so that we are able to become witnesses to the resurrection in our own lives.

This is all laid out clearly in the great and mysterious speeches in John's gospel, chapters fourteen to seventeen. Jesus talks of, 'The Counsellor, the Holy Spirit whom the Father will send in my name' (that is, through the person of Jesus). 'He will teach you all things, and bring to your remembrance all that I have said to you' (14.26), and again, 'He will glorify me, for he will take what is mine and declare it to you' (16.14). The Holy Spirit and the risen Lord are not simply identical, any more than Jesus and the Father are simply identical. There is in both cases a relationship to someone who is other than, and yet the same as, Jesus. For present purposes, we needn't look too hard at the trinitarian aspect yet. Suffice it to say that what the Holy Spirit brings is the whole life and death of the risen Lord, reproducing that life in the lives and deaths of the faithful, so that they become witnesses to that risen life and death. The Holy Spirit is the giving of himself by Jesus, to us to be killed, in obedience to the Father, and the giving back of his life to Jesus by the Father, simultaneously. That is what I think is meant by the Spirit that is in Christ. It is the Spirit of self-giving made present through the concrete human life and death of Jesus. To put it crudely, it is the internal workings of the life and death of Jesus. It is what informed his relationship with the Father, and with us, and the Father's relationship with him and with us. The dynamic that was at work in all that: that is the Holy Spirit.

It is important to grasp that there aren't 'other bits' of the Holy Spirit which we might experience instead, that are separate from, and nothing to do with, the presence of the life and death of the crucified and risen Lord. The Holy Spirit is not some vague, numinous force that is somehow bigger and less exclusive than the crucified and risen Jesus – and rather nicer, perhaps, having to do with peace and joy and so on, rather than murder and violence. The Holy Spirit *is* the Spirit of the crucified and risen Jesus, and any joy, peace, and so on that is genuinely of the Holy Spirit is essentially linked to the presence of the crucified and risen one. Far from being reduced by the link with the crucified and risen Jesus, the Spirit was precisely made maximally present and available because of the crucifixion and resurrection. All the power and self-giving of God that went into the crucifixion and resurrection is perpetually present in the Holy Spirit, and so is perpetually present to all of us who receive it.

Now, from this point on I'm hardly going to mention the Holy Spirit at all. I'd like you to take note of that, and to understand why I've chosen this path. The reason is not because I think it unimportant, or would rather tell the story without it. On the contrary, I think the Holy Spirit is so important that it is in a sense what this book is all about. However, I've chosen to describe the Holy Spirit in a rather different way from what is usual. And this is for a firm reason: for many people, the term 'Holy Spirit' is a comfortingly benign and vague term, a term with no real content or bite on life. If you like, it's God at his most ethereal. If in doubt, attribute it to the Holy Spirit. The Holy Spirit will sort out our tangled petitions and desires and so on. Well, I don't want to deny that. I constantly hope and pray that the Holy Spirit sorts out my tangled petitions and desires. But I do want to bring a little more down to earth, give a little more content to, what the Holy Spirit is about. The Holy Spirit is a divine reality who works on a human level, and our best approach to understanding what goes on is not to let go of the human level, but to allow that level to be deepened. It is not by fleeing the human dimension of our faith, nasty though it be, that we will find God, but by learning how God loves it and transforms it.

It is in the changes in human ways of relating brought about by the presence of the crucified and risen Jesus that we will find out about the Holy Spirit. So I have chosen to talk about these changes without using the word Holy Spirit, to prevent us from flying off into an ethereal realm, and to keep us more firmly tied to how the crucified and risen Lord affects us. It is only thus that we will find out how it is that exactly the same package is available to us with exactly the same force, leading to exactly the same sorts of conversion, or change of heart, as was present to the apostles. That means that just as the risen Lord irrupted into the middle of their lives, in exactly the circumstances in which they were, in the sadness and treachery, and rivalry and fear which characterized them, and started the huge work of their transformation with the *materia prima* that was to hand, so also does he do with us.

Well. That sounds powerful, but in a sense too powerful to be convincing. Before we can get a grip on that, let's start to look at how we humans relate at all, so that we can see where we might begin to experience the life of the risen Lord in our own lives. It's all very well to talk of us having the same faith as the apostles, but sometimes, when people talk like that it sounds as though they're just saying that we ought to believe a lot more than we do, as though we ought to up the supernatural element in our lives, so as to be really good Christians. Well, I don't think that's the case. We can't up the supernatural element in our lives. The whole point of the supernatural is that it can't be upped, or bought, or sold, or bullied or cajoled by us. It can be asked for, even insistently, but that is because, in reality, it can only be given. The authenticity of the supernatural is that it's purely gratuitous.

So in the next chapter I'll begin to look at the human change in knowledge that was brought about by the presence to the apostles of the crucified and risen Lord; the new human understanding about what it is to be human that was brought about by the resurrection. I will look at what I will call the intelligence of the victim.

Questions

1. How do we have access to any knowledge at all about Jesus? What has it taken, in purely human terms, for that knowledge to reach us? What is the 'apostolic witness'?

2. What do you imagine the apostolic group to have been feeling between their abandonment of Jesus and his appearances to them after the resurrection?

3. How do you understand the words 'gratuity' and 'grace'? What is it like to be in the presence of someone who has suffered greatly, but who now is quite without resentment? What does that do to you if you were involved in causing their suffering?

4. How do you understand the phrase 'crucified and risen Lord'? What does it mean that it was the whole of Jesus' life *and* his death which was given back to us in the Resurrection?

5. How were the appearances of Jesus to the apostolic group between the Resurrection and the Ascension different from the experience of the Holy Spirit which came upon that group at Pentecost? How does this help you to understand your own experience of the Holy Spirit?

2
The Intelligence of the Victim

In the last chapter I tried to make available a series of categories by which we can latch on to what happened to the disciples at the resurrection. I stressed the gratuity, the element of forgiveness, the element of mission, and the way in which the risen Lord was the crucified-and-risen Lord. All that is obvious enough. The next step isn't so obvious, and isn't going to be easy for me to express it.

One of the things that happened as a result of the resurrection was a shift in the possibility of human knowledge. That is to say, that before the resurrection of our Lord, there was an area of human life that was radically unknown, maybe even unknowable. And this area of human un-knowing was laid bare, opened up, by the resurrection.

Let me say first what I do not mean. I do not mean that nobody knew there was an afterlife, or a resurrection, and that Jesus' resurrection opened up this whole new unexpected ball game. It is clear that by the time of the Maccabees, elements of popular and, thereafter, Pharisaic Judaism did believe in the resurrection from the dead. You'll remember that Paul got out of a row before the council in Acts 23 by making out that he was being accused by Sadducees of believing something that Pharisees believed anyhow – 'with respect to the hope and the resurrection from the dead I am on trial' – and that got the Pharisees on his side. You'll remember also that Martha believed that Lazarus would be raised on the last day (John 11.24).

It is clear that Jesus' resurrection did reveal the

resurrection, as the Preface for the Second Eucharistic prayer tells us: 'He put an end to death and revealed the resurrection', but not in the sense that it gave us a new bit of information. What it did was to recast the existing belief in the resurrection in the person of Jesus, so that from now on the resurrection was understood to be not something that simply happens next, after death, but something that happens owing to a relationship with the resurrection of Jesus. 'I am the resurrection and the life', says Jesus (John 11.25).

I take it for granted that Jesus' resurrection focalized an understanding of the afterlife – but that is not what I'm interested in pointing out here. I would like to refer to what I mean when I say that something radically new became known by using the phrase, 'the intelligence of the victim'. As a result of the resurrection of Jesus the disciples underwent a profound shift in their understanding, such that they were able to understand something about human life and relationships that had never really been understood before. That something was, to put it simply, the relationship between God and victims.

The gospels are all quite clear on this. Until the resurrection, the disciples did not understand what was going on with Jesus. From the resurrection onwards, they were suddenly able to understand something quite new about Jesus, and about God, and about human beings. The principle evidence for this is that the gospels show simultaneously the non-understanding of the disciples, sometimes the misunderstanding, and at the same time, they show a profound understanding by Jesus of exactly what was going on, where he was going, what was going to happen to him, and why.

Now, these two understandings, present in the same texts, are not there because the disciples didn't understand, but preserved Jesus' words, so that any future generation might be able to understand what was going on. No, the two understandings are there because, after the resurrection, the disciples were able to understand, and could remember the gap between their understanding then, and their understanding now. They were able to tell the story in a new unified way, from the point of view of the risen victim.

Biblical scholars seem to agree that the oldest parts of the gospels are the passion narratives, probably the Marcan passion narrative. Which one came first doesn't matter from the present point of view. What is important is that the disciples started being able to tell the story of Jesus' execution not from the point of view of the muddled, frightened, half-hearted semi-traitors that they all were, but from the point of view of the victim. They could suddenly see that it all made sense. Not 'suddenly' in the sense of in a flash, but rather in the sense of, starting from a fixed point in time – the resurrection.

They were able to go back over all the events that they had witnessed, and taken part in, and see what was really happening, all along, to which they had been blind at the time. They give evidence of this in the first place in their use of Old Testament quotes to show how what had seemed like a bloody mess was in fact the necessary fulfilment of prophecy. So, in Mark's gospel, they were able to see in the passion the fulfilment of the psalm of abandonment, number twenty-two, starting, 'My God, My God, why hast thou forsaken me', as well as the section of the book of Wisdom (2.12–24) which starts, 'Let us lie in wait for the righteous man', and goes on, 'for if the righteous man is God's son, he will help him', and many other passages of the Old Testament.

John's gospel gives even more obvious evidence of this, by quoting Scriptures which were being fulfilled: so, as the soldiers parted Jesus' garment, 'this was to fulfil the scripture, 'They parted my garments among them, and for my clothing they cast lots' (John 19.24, quoting Ps. 22.18), and again (John 19.36), 'These things took place that the Scripture might be fulfilled, "Not a bone of him shall be broken", and again another scripture says, "they shall look on him whom they have pierced"'.

Now, it is important to understand that when the disciples started seeing the fulfilment of scriptural prophecy in the events surrounding the execution of Jesus, it was not that they said to themselves, 'Gosh, Scripture has been fulfilled: and here are the proof texts'. No, rather, they had understood something radically new about the whole way in which God makes himself manifest to humanity, and were finding a golden thread of hints of this radical new discovery in Old Testament prophecy. We are told as much when the risen Jesus speaks to the disciples on the road to Emmaus, and says, '"O foolish men, and slow of heart to believe all that the prophets have spoken! Was it not necessary that the Christ should suffer these things, and enter into his glory?" And beginning with Moses and all the prophets, he interpreted to them in all the Scriptures the things concerning himself' (Luke 24.26-7).

It was this that enabled them to go back in their memories and tell the story of Jesus as that of the self-giving, and self-revealing victim, who alone knew what was really going on. First of all they were able to tell the story of his passion in this way. The evidence for this is in the early preaching of Peter in Acts. Peter's first speeches are full of Old Testament references showing an understanding of the crucifixion as the rejection by Israel of God's Holy One, done in ignorance; the resurrection offers Israel an opportunity to be forgiven, and to be brought out of ignorance concerning God and sin. Time and again in the New Testament we come across the phrase 'The stone rejected by the builders has become the head of the corner'. The quotation is from Psalm 118, and would have been known to all those involved. Its meaning has suddenly come alive, as it is seen to reveal how the whole edifice of the understanding of Israel as God's chosen people is recast, starting from the expelled victim.

So, the making of this man a victim, apparently in ignorance, and done to please God (Jesus had been judged a blasphemer) was in fact the condition which made it possible for God to be revealed for what he really is: the forgiving victim. This is the great irony present in all the gospels, and particularly in Luke and Acts: that by killing the Messiah, Israel was, without being aware of it, offering up the sacrifice of all sacrifices to God, the sacrifice that could become the basis for their salvation.

It is interesting to see how this understanding, the perception, or what I have called the intelligence of the victim, is slowly read back into the living memory of those who had been with Jesus, and who had preserved his sayings, whether by memory, or by writing them down. For all the gospels show the life of Jesus leading up to the passion. It is not as though he lived his life, and then by mistake got involved in an imbroglio in Jerusalem and so got killed. From the vantage point of the resurrection, the presence of the forgiving victim, the disciples could see that the whole drift of Jesus' life had been towards the passion.

Now please note what I am *not* saying here. I am not saying that as a result of the resurrection, the disciples invented a whole set of stories about Jesus as their way of explaining the resurrection. The texts manifestly are not *about* the disciples' new self-understanding, even though they do reveal that the disciples did now understand things anew. The gospels all bear witness to Jesus himself having understood all this from the beginning. That is precisely what the disciples did not understand before Jesus' death, and did understand after his resurrection. They all bear witness to the fact that, unlike themselves, Jesus had what I have called 'the intelligence of the victim' from the beginning.

There are certain obvious pieces of evidence for this, such as the way in which Jesus prophesies his own forthcoming death to the disciples – passages like this from Mark 9.31-2: 'For he was teaching his disciples, saying to them, "The Son of man will be delivered into the hands of men, and they will kill him; and when he is killed, after three days he will rise." But they did not understand the saying, and they were afraid to ask him'. These make explicit that Jesus knew where he was going, and what was to happen. They bear witness to the fact that the intelligence of the victim was not simply a post-resurrection understanding, but one which Jesus had all along. Jesus' understanding had probably been nourished by the texts of the Old Testament as well: it is probable that he based his understanding of the resurrection, and indeed his hope in it, on the text of Hosea 6.1-2 which was to be so important to the disciples after the resurrection: 'Come let us return to the Lord, for he has torn that he may heal us; he has stricken, and he will bind us up. After two days he will revive us; on the third day he will raise us up, that we may live before him'.

The texts bear witness to Jesus having had a profound and original new understanding of the sacred texts of Judaism before his execution. These texts accompanied his acting in ways that he knew would result in his being killed. The texts also bear witness to his teaching his disciples about this, and their not understanding it. This is terribly important, since it means that what I have called the 'intelligence of the victim' is not only a post-resurrection intelligence. It was a pre-resurrection intelligence in Jesus alone, not understood at all by the disciples, and, at one stage, actively impeded by Peter (see the famous 'Get thee behind me, Satan' passage).

What did happen at the resurrection was that precisely the intelligence of Scripture, and of the relationship between God and victim that Jesus had beforehand, came also to be held by the disciples, such that they could understand what they hadn't been able to before. I ask you to consider how completely unique this is: if you or I take part in an historical event - let us say, the lynching of Ceauçescu - thereafter, the story we tell is of the sort 'Ceauçescu, my part in his downfall'. We tell what we did, or didn't do, whether we were right to do so or not, how we would have acted if such and such, what we said to Ceauçescu on the way to the firing squad, what Mrs Ceauçescu said to our mate when he picked up her handbag. The story would be the story of our involvement in the passion of Nicolae and Elena, not the story of the inner understanding of what was going on from the point of view of the victims of the lynch. We might speculate on what they felt like, on how they attempted to relate the last tumultuous hours of their lives with the previous sixty or seventy years. However, the whole pattern of their lives, supposing that there was a clear one, would not have been manifest to us at all.

Yet that is the story that the disciples are telling: the story of the lynch from the point of view of the victim's own understanding of what was going on before the lynch happened, up to, and during it. That is to say, they, the disciples, are not in the centre of the story, the victim is, and it is the victim's intelligence that is allowed to provide the lines which make the story what it is.

Now that is something of what I mean by 'the intelligence of the victim'. However to stop there would only be half the story, or rather less than half. It would suggest that what we have is the story of a unique individual, who had a special sort of knowledge about how he was going to be killed, who lived it out, and afterwards his disciples understood it all, thanks to his resurrection. That would make of Jesus a 'special man', a magic figure with an arcane knowledge – the intelligence of the victim – that a select group of initiates can later get hold of.

What makes the intelligence of the victim which the disciples received as a result of the resurrection even more remarkable, was that it did not only yield them information about Jesus and his self-awareness. It revealed to them the fulness of the drift of what he had been teaching *them* while they were with him. What Jesus had been teaching was perfectly plain and public. And yet, it was as though they had had a veil over their understanding, and were unable to grasp what it was about. That is to say, that all along, there was nothing arcane or occult about the intelligence of the victim: Jesus had been trying to make it as plain as day. The drama was that Jesus was revealing something about which human knowledge is always shrouded in self-deception. Something, if you like, which goes beyond the roots of what makes us aware.

The only way I think I can explain this is with reference to personal experience. I hope that we have all had the experience of gradually coming to perceive exactly the same things in a different way. We look out at a certain reality, at home, at work, in a relationship, and realize that, without our having understood a particular fact, or circumstance that we didn't before, nevertheless, we are aware that our whole way of looking has changed profoundly and subtly. This might be for any number of reasons, like a new friendship, or the end of a period of anxiety where we hadn't realized how much we'd allowed it to colour our vision. The point is that the change is not in our conscious awareness, but in the background to that, in what makes us have a conscious awareness at all. It is as though we are watching a film; the film doesn't change, but the projectionist subtly puts a filter into the projector, so that exactly the same film comes out, but is changed into sepia, or pink, or whatever.

The point of my bringing this out is that the disciples' block to understanding the intelligence of the victim was at this level. It was not a question of stupidity, of not grasping certain basic teachings. The problem was for them, and is for us, that the intelligence that was in Jesus was an intelligence at the level of what makes us conscious, what makes us aware. The disciples had, as we have, a background to understanding, which is actually formed by what Jesus was trying to change. The filter, if you like, which colours our perception without our being aware of it, not only is not the same as Jesus' intelligence of the victim, but is in fact its reverse: our programming, if you like, forms us in rivalry, and the techniques of survival by exclusion.

None of this, it must be said, could have been known until after the resurrection, when the new intelligence was able to irrupt into the lives of the disciples. However, they did then understand that Jesus had been trying to make this available to them not only in the way he went to his death, but in all the things he had taught them. I'd like to look at the way Jesus made available to his disciples this intelligence of the victim, and the way they were able to see the wholeness of what he taught and how he died. I'd like to do this by looking at three particular areas of Jesus' teaching: concerning moral issues, concerning discipleship, and concerning the foundation of the new Israel, or the coming of the kingship of God.

Matthew's gospel is, famously, the gospel where Jesus' moral teaching is presented at its fullest. Now, remember from what vantage point this teaching is given us: the disciples, their understanding made alive by the presence to them of the crucified-and-risen Lord, are bearing witness to Jesus' teaching. That is to say, they are reporting what they heard, but from the point of view which they have now come to acquire - where they understand its inner logic. Every one of the New Testament writings has this form: it is written either by one of the apostolic witnesses to the resurrection, or by someone intimately connected with one of those witnesses, who learnt what they wrote down from one or more of the witnesses. The New Testament is the putting into writing of the apostolic witness to the resurrection.

Among the things to which the apostles bear witness through these writings was the tremendous impact which Jesus' teaching made when it was first delivered, that is, before Jesus' death: 'the crowds were astonished at his teaching, for he taught them as one who had authority, and not as their scribes' (Matt. 7.28-9).

Now, the teaching of the Sermon on the Mount points to what I have called 'the intelligence of the victim'. It starts with the beatitudes, where the people chosen as exemplars of proximity to God are all marginal, dependent people. People who have a certain relationship to others which one might describe as precarious: the poor in spirit are poor relative to people who might use power and riches against them, those who mourn are those who are in a relationship of vulnerability owing either to some loss, or some overbearing situation, the meek are meek in the midst of a social other that despises meekness, the merciful refuse to be involved in a vengeful relation to the other, that is they don't insist on their rights over against another, the pure in heart have acquired their purity of heart with difficulty in the midst of a world which does not encourage it, the peacemakers are notoriously those who eventually get blamed by both sides for not sharing their violence - each side sees them as traitors and those who are persecuted for righteousness . . . well the intelligence of the victim couldn't be more explicit - and this is emphasized again in the final beatitude: 'Blessed are you when men revile you and persecute you, and utter all kinds of falsehood against you'.

The key feature of blessedness is that it involves living a deliberately chosen and cultivated sort of life which is not involved in the power and violence of the world, and which because of this fact, makes the ones living it immensely vulnerable to being turned into victims. That is the centre of the ethic as taught by Jesus in the Sermon on the Mount. If we then turn to the end of Jesus' last discourse before his passion – the mirror image of this, the first of his discourses – we find the same intelligence at work. In the famous passage of the last judgement, the judgement is defined not in terms of belonging to this or that group, or believing this or that dogma. The judgement is presented in terms of the human relationship towards victims. Those who hunger, thirst, are naked, sick, or imprisoned. Those who have understood, whether or not they know anything about Jesus, are those who have seen their way out of the self-deception of the world which is blind to its victims, and have reached out to help them. Again, the intelligence of the victim: it is the crucified and risen victim who is the judge of the world, and the world is judged in the light of its relationship to the crucified and risen victim.

Now what is extraordinary about this intelligence, particularly in Matthew's gospel, is that it is universal. The intelligence of the victim is not seen as something only related to the person of Jesus, though he reveals it fully; it is seen as something that has always been present. Jesus is revealing something that has always been true about human society, from the time of Abel the just, to that of Zechariah the son of Berachiah (Matt. 23.35). That is, from the beginnings of humanity, until the last of the prophets in the Bible as it then was. Human society is a violent place, which makes victims, and the revelation of God is to be found in the midst of that violence, on the side of the victims.

Again let me stress that this intelligence was made

available to the disciples after, and as a result of, the appearances of the crucified and risen Lord. The intelligence however is not limited to the very many and frequent passages where, especially in Matthew, Jesus actually talks about persecution - his own, or that which the disciples will undergo. It is to be found at one remove in all the moral teaching!

Let's go back to the Sermon on the Mount. After the beatitudes, Jesus gives a series of teachings which reveal the way in which humans are utterly constituted in violence - anger is the equivalent of killing, lust the equivalent of adultery, a quarrel with a brother the complete invalidation of an act of worship of God. Because of this, the law, which Jesus does not come to abolish, does not go far enough. Jesus is determined to teach people at the level the law cannot reach: how to be free from being bound into the other by violence: so, no retribution to the other who violates you, because if you do, you remain on the same level as that person - so instead, turn the other cheek, walk the extra mile. It is only by not being stuck at the level of reacting to the violent other that we are free. Move out of reciprocally violent relationships, and into free ones. The strictures against false piety and hypocrisy are because the ones who practise those things are tied into what other people think, they are not able to act freely. They are run by the opinion, or what they hope to be the opinion of the other. Hence the tremendous importance of forgiveness, or loosing the bonds which tie one in to the violent other. For only thus can one be free, and perfect as the heavenly Father is perfect.

Yet it is precisely this freedom, which is to be the mark of the follower of Christ, which prepares the follower to become the victim. This aspect of the intelligence of the victim is vital. For it is this freedom which lays bare the workings of human society, and that society reacts against it by expelling it and persecuting it. At the same time the freedom comes prior to the victimization. Let me try to explain that. If you take the phrase 'the intelligence of the victim' you might think that I am talking about some kind of victim-complex, or paranoia. I might be saying that Christianity was simply a huge version of this complex, which can be found in all societies, and in almost all humans, at least under certain circumstances. But that is exactly what is *not* meant by 'the intelligence of the victim'. The intelligence of the victim comes from a freedom in giving oneself to others, in not being moved by the violence of others, even when it perceives that this free self-giving is going to be lynched as a result.

The free self-giving is not a seeking to be lynched, but is completely open-eyed about the probability of just this happening. However, not even the natural fear of this is enough to shake the freedom that is based on a continual loosing, forgiving, of the violence of the other's relationship to the free self-giver. Now, the evidence is that Jesus taught, before, and on his way up to, his execution, exactly this sort of open-eyed freedom-towards-being-lynched, and indeed that this is the whole drift of his moral teaching. He taught people how to loosen themselves from relationships of violence with each other, where their personalities were constituted by the reciprocal give and take of that violence, and instead to start to side with the victims and those who can easily be victimized, even though, as an inevitable consequence of this breaking out of the violent determinism of the world, they would be liable to become victims themselves.

Let me recap: the intelligence of the victim is the discovery of the sort of human beings we are, and how we tend to build our personal and social identities on a series of exclusions. The discovery was and is made possible because Jesus had the intelligence of the victim from the beginning. After the resurrection the disciples began to see the internal coherence between his teaching, and the way he had lived, leading up to his

death. That is to say, the intelligence of the victim that
had been in Jesus, passed to them. They began to be
able to understand the story of Jesus' life from Jesus'
own point of view. Now, this, the intelligence of the
victim in the disciples, was not, I think, an immediate
flash, but a process of understanding, to which the
gospel texts give witness. You may be worried by what
appears to be an excessive concentration on the theme
of the victim, as though I am making out that to be a
victim is in itself a good thing. Nothing could be further
from my meaning. Please remember that I am not
trying to give a simple abstract account of some topics
of our faith, but rather to explore the process by which
the disciples came to understand Jesus as a result of the
resurrection. This approach is designed so that we can
have some pegs on which to hang any approach to the
question of how we know Jesus, which is what this
book is pointing towards.

So let me illustrate further what I mean by the
intelligence of the victim which came to the disciples.
The gospels witness to the way in which Jesus knew
that the authorities, variously described as chief priests,
elders, scribes or Pharisees, were at various times
plotting against him, to get rid of him. He is shown as
revealing to them exactly what they were doing in a
series of teachings, such as the parable of the murderous
tenants of the vineyard. But Jesus was not only
revealing to them their behaviour with regard to his
person, he was also establishing the criterion for
understanding the kingdom of God: in running their
vineyard on the basis of the exclusion of others,
prophets and the Son, they missed the whole point of
the vineyard, which would be taken over by people who
would build *from* the excluded victim, not by excluding
the victim. For that is how God makes himself known
among humans. This is the density in Jesus' quotation
to the Pharisees of the line from Psalm 118, 'The very
stone which the builders rejected has become the head

of the corner; this was the Lord's doing and it is marvellous in our eyes'.

Again, just to show that what Jesus is revealing is not merely the hidden motives behind the conflict between himself and the Pharisees, but something beyond that, look at the 'woes to the scribes and Pharisees' in Matthew 23. This is a passage about missing the point. It gradually builds up from an attack on what might be taken as isolated examples of the distorted religious observance of a particular caste, to linking that sort of religion to a blindness about involvement in building a society on murder. I quoted already the verse about the blood of the innocent Abel, showing that the criticism was universal. The pain behind the denunciation is precisely that the heirs of Moses *ought to have known* and understood the terrible way in which human societies work by basing their social order on victims; if they had been faithful to Moses, they would have understood, and been the builders and constructors of a society which did not do that. Their society, based on the victim people expelled from Egypt, should precisely not have been like the other nations. Jesus' painful denunciation was exactly because Israel was behaving like the nations, and therefore its strict observance of the law, far from doing what the law was meant to do – create a society in which there were no victims or victimizable people, where widows and orphans and exiles and sojourners were honoured – was simply a piece of whitewashing covering over the same victimizing violence as happened everywhere else.

To see this denunciation as simply an attack on the Pharisees is to miss the point: it is a revelation that the Pharisees are betraying their sacred task of constructing God's kingdom, and have become the same as all other religions – clothed in veils of self-delusion about their involvement in violence. It is a denunciation made out of pain – ending in the great cry, 'O Jerusalem

Jerusalem, killing the prophets and stoning those who are sent to you! How often would I have gathered your children together as a hen gathers her brood under her wings, and you would not! Behold, your house is forsaken and desolate'.

So, the intelligence of the victim is not only the criterion for the moral life of the Christian, moving into freedom and thus running the risk of becoming a victim, but it is also the criterion from which Jesus judges and criticizes the religious practices of humanity, that is, the human construction of social order. However, it is not only that, and here I tread on very difficult ground. It sounds as though the intelligence of the victim might be simply a negative thing, a strategy for coping with a wicked world. It is in fact more than that.

I indicated that Jesus' moral teaching was about freedom, that is, the demand that we work out from a series of reactive, reciprocating relationships, to be able to act freely. It is this which makes it possible to side with human victims, that makes its practiser him or herself a likely candidate for victimage. The intelligence of the victim is a consequence of something which precedes it – that is, the teaching about freedom. It is fascinating to observe how in the gospels the disciples were able to discern this back in the life of Jesus from their new perspective of people touched by the resurrection. It was not, as they could see, having been killed that made Jesus special, or even having been killed and raised again. It was what, for want of a better term, I call the free self-giving of Jesus, which led to his being crucified.

That is to say, the life of human freedom leading to persecution which Jesus was teaching his disciples was first led by him, and it was this free self-giving that made him special. I would even go so far as to say that this was the sign that they had had among them a man who was also God. As the disciples' intelligence of the victim deepened, so they saw the self-giving as prior to the passion. So, Luke and Matthew take us back beyond Jesus' public ministry to the infancy, and illustrate the given-ness of Jesus even as an infant. Luke characteristically emphasizes the graciousness of the given in Jesus: the angels, the child in the Temple, but keeps alive the threat of the sword in Simeon's prophecy to Mary. Matthew characteristically portrays Jesus' infancy as a series of near escapes from lynch deaths - Mary was not stoned thanks to an angel telling Joseph to take her as wife even though she was pregnant, Herod did not manage to massacre Jesus, who had escaped to Egypt; yet Jesus was clearly given as a fulfilment of the prophecy concerning Emmanuel. Notice how the intelligence of the victim reaches right back into the family life of Jesus.

John, as in so many places, makes this intelligence even clearer than the other evangelists - having probably had longer to think about it. He places the givenness outside history and in God. So, in the famous verse, 'For God so loved the world that he gave his only Son . . .' (John 3.16), a verse which contains echoes of Abraham's near-sacrifice of Isaac, the Abrahamic sacrifice is turned on its head. God gives his Son, out of love for the world, which sacrifices him. In the intelligence of the victim, the self-giving is prior, anterior to the sacrifice, and the sacrifice is incidental, accidental, to the self-giving. So, Jesus did not give himself so as to be a victim, he gave himself, in the full awareness that he was to be a victim, but did not want this at all. There was no death-wish in Jesus. This is why John stresses particularly Jesus' freedom with relation to his 'hour' - he deliberately avoided lynching on several occasions because his hour had not yet come. He is also completely in command at his passion, and even says so beforehand: 'For this reason the Father loves me, because I lay down my life that I may take it again. No one takes it from me, but I lay it down of my own accord' (John 10.18).

Of course, most spectacularly, this intelligence of the victim is present in John's prologue, where the word by which all things were created, and its coming into the world, are all prior to the victimization, which is passed through with a single phrase, 'He came to his own home, and his own people received him not'. In John's gospel more than in any other, the self-giving of God is stressed as the key behind the victimization. The resurrection of the crucified and risen one had given the complete background to the self-giving victim, showing everything as depending on the self-giving and revealing of God. It is this movement, and this alone, that made possible the emergence of the discovery that God is Love. It was this which made it possible that Jesus' self-giving as victim came to be understood to be part of the self-giving of God, which hugely anteceded it.

If you doubt this interpretation, look at 1 John 4.7-11. There it is set out in black and white: God is love, this was manifest in God sending his Son into the world, as an expiation for our sins. It is the revolution wrought by the intelligence of the victim that was made available to the disciples after the resurrection of the crucified and risen Lord that made it possible for the discovery to be made that God is love. The phrase, 'God is love' is only possible within the intelligence of the victim. It is not an abstract definition, it is part of the revelation of the crucified and risen one.

Let's now turn back from these giddying matters to the intelligence of the victim in Jesus' teaching on discipleship. Of course, this is part of the same package as his moral teaching, but looked at from a slightly different angle.

After the resurrection, and because of the suicide of Judas, the apostles meet in Acts 1 to choose a successor to Judas, so that the full number of twelve apostles may be maintained - the number that, as we will see, signified the new Israel that Jesus had founded. The criterion for the choice of the candidates was that they be men 'who have accompanied us during all the time that the Lord Jesus went in and out among us, beginning from the baptism of John until the day when he was taken up from us – one of these men must become with us a witness to his resurrection' (Acts 1.21-2). So already Peter understood, in the light of the crucified and risen Lord, that to occupy the official role of witness, it was necessary to have witnessed the life leading up to the death as well as the resurrection. That means that the apostles now understood that the whole of their discipleship had been a preparation for being able to bear witness to the resurrection. What they had been doing all along was suddenly made clear to them, which it hadn't been before.

The tale they tell, then, in the gospels, with regard to their discipleship, is the story of how they were called and led on, and taught by this man Jesus, being prepared to be living witnesses to the intelligence of the victim when Jesus was no longer among them. It is the story of which the key term is *skandalon*, or stumbling block. Following Jesus meant learning not to be scandalized by him, not to be caused to stumble. This was within the context of a long Jewish tradition of the importance of avoiding giving scandal to other people, a notion which seems quaint to us, but which is still very much alive in, for example, the Muslim insistence on the veil for women, which is meant to prevent luring men into occasions of sin.

Jesus was teaching his disciples how to imitate him in everything he did – preaching, casting out demons, praying, healing the sick, and so on. Time and again he is careful to insist that no element of rivalry creep in – the disciple is not above his master (Luke 6.40) – and yet he insists that ones believing in him will do greater works than he has done, because he is going to the Father (John 14.12). He gives, in John's gospel, the ultimate reason behind this non-rivalistic imitation – the completely pacific imitation of his Father: he does

everything he sees his Father do. He presents himself
as one who imitates his Father in all things; this is his
obedience.

So the disciple must learn to follow him, which means
learning to overcome stumbling blocks. Now, to do a
proper study of the notion of stumbling block in the
New Testament would far outstrip the bounds of this
book – because the notion is far more often present
than the words *skandalon* and *skandalizesthai* would
suggest. What I would like to offer is the basis, to be
found in the presence to the disciples of the crucified
and risen Lord, by which they came to an understanding
of the *skandalon* as being the obstacle not only to
discipleship in the immediate sense of physically
following this man, Jesus, but also as being the obstacle
which pervades human relationships, and which must
be overcome if we are to be the people we are made to be.

The great line about 'scandal', which has become well
known, comes in Paul's first letter to the Corinthians.
There he says, 'but we preach Christ crucified, a
stumbling block [Greek: *skandalon*] to the Jews and
folly to Gentiles' (1 Cor. 1.23). Now this means that one
of the effects of the resurrection on the disciples was
that it removed the *skandalon*, without taking it away.
Which is another way of saying what I have tried to
say earlier, that Jesus was present as crucified Lord
who was risen. The stumbling block was how to follow
someone who had died. How to follow someone who had
ended in failure. This takes us back to the disciples on
Easter Saturday. They were scandalized, stymied. They
had believed in, and followed this man, had allowed his
teaching to permeate every area of their lives, and they
had trusted in his ability to produce a powerful victory
over his enemies, and establish the kingdom of God in
Israel. They had been scandalized by his failure to
do this.

The resurrection made present the crucified Lord, the
failed one, as living. That is, it removed the scandal,

without taking away the death. In fact it made the dead alive as a sign that there was no scandal. It took away the last stumbling block to following Jesus, or any man, that is, the separation brought about by that man's death. This enabled them to look again at the process by which Jesus had taught them. Remember that Jesus had constantly prevented the disciples from being scandalized at his teaching, he had taken them aside and explained his teaching in private. The gospels are full of accounts of other people who were caused to stumble by Jesus' teaching. Take for instance the rich young man who went away grieving when he discovered that perfection meant leaving his riches and following Jesus – it meant getting rid of something which would cause him to stumble. He preferred to stick by his stumbling block, and not follow Jesus. Remember all those who went away when Jesus taught that he was the true bread, and that he would give his flesh for the life of the world. They were caused to stumble. Jesus brought his disciples through these scandals – even if only by the skin of their teeth. Remember that after that speech, the disciples were the only ones who did not go away, and he asked them whether they weren't going too. Peter replied, 'Lord, to whom shall we go? You have the words of eternal life' (John 6.68).

However, Jesus could not protect his disciples from what he knew would be the ultimate scandal – his forthcoming lynch death. Of course, he warned them on every possible occasion, producing reactions from Peter which were indicative of Peter's having been scandalized – on the one hand, 'God forbid, Lord! This shall never happen to you' (Matt. 16.22), and on the other, 'Even though they all fall away, I will not' (Mark 14.29). Peter first denied that the scandal would happen, thus making himself a stumbling block to Jesus, and then, when he saw that a time of trial would come, he promised not to be scandalized by it. This was a promise that his following would not be interrupted by it, a promise which he couldn't deliver. Jesus knew that no one would be able to follow him through the scandal of a death which must inevitably seem a failure, because it was written, 'I will strike the shepherd, and the sheep will be scattered' (Mark 14.27).

What he gave the disciples on his resurrection, therefore, was the ability to follow him without death being a stumbling block. There was nothing left that might cause his disciples to stumble - death was swallowed up in victory. Now, see what this led them to understand: it led them to understand that all stumbling blocks - all relations where people are locked in with each other as stumbling blocks, where imitation and learning is distorted by rivalry - are related to death. The presence to them of the crucified and risen Lord was what enabled them to learn to imitate pacifically, having the deepest bonds of their relationships which were cast in modes of stumbling, loosed, so that they might no longer live towards death, but instead live with death as an incidental side issue.

Again, it is the intelligence of the victim given after the resurrection that enables them to see the whole of this healing process of discipleship in its light. It is this which enables them to see the point of the very mysterious utterance in John's gospel: 'It is to your advantage that I go away, for if I do not go away the Counsellor will not come to you, but if I go, I will send him to you'. The suggestion here is that Jesus could, as a human being present with the disciples, teach them only so much. He could teach them many elements of following him, they could become authentic imitators of him, doing the works he did, just as he did the works of his Father, by his perfect imitation of him. That is, Jesus could exercise a certain sort of trance-like hold upon his disciples. But it could only go so far. There were two things militating against the imitation being complete, the possession being full. The first was that Jesus was a human being like his disciples, and therefore was other to them as any human being is to another - and thus not able to move them completely as his Father was. The Father is other than each one of us on a completely different level from us. He can thus move our freedoms, our will and our intellect, without displacing them, as humans do to each other when we teach, command, bully, or attract each other. Jesus, because he was a human being, could not, at least until he was killed, completely possess his disciples.

The second reason that the disciples' imitation of Jesus could not be complete while he was still alive was that in any human relation, the knowledge that death will supervene, will separate, is an ultimate factor, one that cannot be bypassed. There is always, in any human relationship of dedication, an element of the provisional because of the certainty of death. We are all, rightly, suspicious of leaders, or whoever, who exercise the ability to command loyalty even to the death. This is because it is usually the death of the followers that is involved, not that of the commander! So, there is a certain stumbling block to a perfect imitation posed by the simple fact of being a human this side of death. This was removed by the resurrection. The presence of the crucified and risen Lord made available the possibility of a perfect human imitation of Jesus, because it made available an imitation without the stumbling block of death, and with the possibility of the possession of the disciple by Jesus at the level of freedom. That is to say, after the period of Jesus' physical appearances, he was no longer 'other' to the disciples as we are to each other, but was 'other' only in the way that God is, beyond the possibility of rivalry, who moves us from within, to will and to work. For the first time a human imitation became possible that need have no element of rivalry.

In the light of this, it is possible to see how the disciples came to understand the relationship between the stumbling block of Jesus' death, which had been a

stumbling block for them until it was overcome by the
resurrection, and all the stumbling blocks which men
and women put in each other's way. Precisely because
we desire to be, to live, we cannot imitate each other
pacifically, and thus learn from each other, but always
have to get ahead so as to avoid death. So, we cannot
be gratuitous with each other, but always have to insist
on rights, on everyone getting what they deserve, on
not doing more than we have to. Our imitation, which is
the only way as humans we learn, from our tenderest
infancy upwards, is always provisional, because we are
only doing it for our advantage, which we would quickly
use against our teacher if the need arose, and so we
guarantee our sense of being by an imitation turned
rivalistic, which locks us into all sorts of conflicts. At
the bottom of this spiral is death. Ultimately, all our
imitation is based on a desire for being, for life, to
which we will sacrifice anything, even as far as killing.
Of course, we disguise this from ourselves in a variety
of ways – but never very convincingly. We need wars,
we need starvation in third world countries, we need
other people to die so that we can live.

Learning to follow Jesus is learning how to receive
the gift of life, of being, which we inescapably desire, as
something given, something which can only be received
by a non-rivalistic, a pacific imitation of someone, who
makes this imitation possible by being beyond death.
So the disciples were able to see how they had been
slowly summoned out of living in rivalry: Jesus put a
small child in their midst to show who the greatest was
in the kingdom of heaven; he insisted that greatness
meant following him to death, it meant being amongst
others as one who serves. All these measures add up to
an ascesis of desire. It is a question of moving human
desire out of a pattern of relating to others from rivalry,
a relationship based on death, to a relationship based
on the pacific imitation of Jesus, leading to a relationship with others of gratuity, service. This is only

possible from the security of having received life
gratuitously. It is possible to go through the gospels
and see exactly how this intelligence is omnipresent.
On the one hand there is to be found pacific imitation
avoiding victimization, but making one a candidate for
becoming a victim, and on the other hand, rivalistic
imitation leading one to avoid being a victim, but
making others one's victims.

Just to give one example, one that is not usually
quoted under this particular set of circumstances, let us
look at John 10, and the discourse about the good
shepherd. Here you have the sheep following the
shepherd - the ultimate picture of non-rivalistic following, of pacific imitation. The sheep hear his voice and
follow him, but what makes him the good shepherd is
precisely that he is able to lay down his life for his
sheep. That is, it is possible to imitate him beyond
death. He does not cause his sheep scandal, as do other
shepherds, who run away when danger is near. They
cannot be safely imitated, but are thieves and hirelings,
because they themselves are scandalized by death,
which they have not overcome. Between the good
shepherd and the sheep there is a connatural knowledge,
because there is no stumbling block, no rivalistic
imitation. The whole complex of ideas about pacific
imitation, the scandal of death being overcome, and
death being the scandal for others could not be more
tightly expressed than in John 10.27-8: 'My sheep hear
my voice, and I know them, and they follow me; and I
give them eternal life, and they shall never perish, and
no one shall snatch them out of my hand'. It's all there:
the understanding of discipleship that had been made
clear in the light of the risen victim.

When Jesus uses the language of 'shepherd' he is of
course using for himself one of the titles which Israel
reserved for God - 'Shepherd of Israel, hear us'. Thus
there is already present the idea that his human person,
by permitting this entirely pacific imitation, is on the

same level in relation to us as is God. That is, Jesus is able, by leading us in our imitation, to possess us and move us as God is. He says as much in the next verses: 'My Father who has given them to me is greater than all, and no one is able to snatch them out of the Father's hand. I and the Father are one' (John 10.29–30). It is precisely this assertion that leads the crowd to seek to stone him. That is to say: because people are locked into a stumbling block with relation to each other and to God, they react to the possibility of a completely pacific imitation as to a scandal, and seek to lynch it. In this scene we see brought together with magnificent clarity the two elements of the intelligence of the victim that I have been discussing in this chapter: the intelligence of the victim living towards the knowledge of being lynched, on the one hand; and on the other, the way in which the intelligence of the victim has opened up the understanding of what Jesus was teaching his disciples as to the nature of discipleship, and simultaneously, the nature of the world of scandal in which we live, the whole area which a later theology was to call 'original sin'.

So, let me sum up where we have reached: we looked in the first chapter at Jesus' resurrection. Since then we have been looking at the intelligence of the victim, which that made possible. In the next chapter I'd like to look at the way in which the intelligence of the victim went worldwide, because it is that that will give us, I hope, the basis of a chance to work out, in the final chapter, what 'knowing Jesus' might mean today.

Questions

1. The 'intelligence of the victim' is an odd phrase. What do you think it means? How does a serene potential victim reconnoitre the territory in which he or she is going to make a stand for

the truth? Do you have an experience of acting with this intelligence? Do you know any stories about people who have?

2. What had slowly to begin to be undone in the apostolic group for them to be able to grasp what Jesus had been on about before his crucifixion?

3. Can you think of an event, or a story, which is usually told from the perspective of the lynchers, but which you can begin to understand from the perspective of the victim? Can your own experience of your school playground be recast in this light?

4. What does it mean for your understanding of moral questions if these are looked at from the point of view of one on his or her way to being cast out? How does this perspective change your reading of the Sermon on the Mount?

5. What is a scandal? How does our daily use of the word differ from the New Testament's use of 'skandalon'? What does it mean to say that Jesus made possible a non-scandalized following of himself by removing the scandal of death?

3

The Universal Victim

In the previous chapter, I have tried to bring out the way in which the presence to the disciples of the crucified and risen Lord introduced them into what I called the intelligence of the victim, and how this intelligence included the laying bare of aspects of being human which had never been fully known before, except by Jesus. I tried to bring out the way in which it is exactly Jesus' intelligence of the world (what Paul would call 'the mind of Christ') which was made available to the disciples after the resurrection. It was this which enabled the disciples to understand what had been going on, and to deepen their understanding of what Jesus had been teaching and showing them. Thus they were able faithfully to reconstruct Jesus' moral teaching, and his teaching about discipleship, from their present understanding, an insight which the risen victim had made apparent to them. I tried to show the internal coherence between the gospel teachings on these matters, and the intelligence of the victim that was made available to the disciples after the resurrection.

There is, however, at least a third area in which Jesus' intelligence of the victim became clear to the disciples after the resurrection, and that is Jesus' teaching concerning the foundation of the new Israel, or the coming of the kingdom of God. Again, what is important is the evidence of an internal coherence between the intelligence of the victim, and the huge change of understanding, to which the New Testament texts bear witness, which made it possible for the idea of the chosen people of Israel to become that of the new Israel, a universal, non-racial, non-geographical category.

As a prelude to discussing this, let me try and remove a possible illusion into which some people are induced by the New Testament texts. There are four obvious categories of texts in the New Testament. The gospels, the epistles, the acts of the apostles, and the apocalypse. Now, of these, the gospels and the book of Acts seem to be giving an historical account of significant events in the past, while the epistles, and in a more grandiose way, the apocalypse, seem to be dealing with the situation of the present, and perhaps of the future. Now, the possible illusion is this: that we look at the events and their significance in a linear way starting with the infancy narratives in those gospels that contain them, and finishing up with the apocalypse and its sweep of history and the future.

This perfectly natural way of looking at the texts seems to me to miss out on the rather important way in which whether they look back, or forward, or at the present situation, essentially the same intelligence of the victim can be seen to be the formative structure of the regard cast by each text. All the New Testament texts are post-resurrection documents which have as the touchstone by which they interpret the reality they seek to treat, the same intelligence made present by the crucified-and-risen Lord. This is precisely what constitutes them as part of the apostolic witness, and is the basis for their inclusion in the canon: what makes them the norm of the faith of the Church.

I mention this, since it may not be immediately obvious that exactly the same intelligence of the victim underlies the understanding of Jesus' life and death in the gospels, his moral teaching and his teaching of discipleship, as underlies Paul's approach to the community problems in Corinth, his teaching on the relationship between Israel and the Gentiles in Romans, his teaching on the gracious nature of justification. It is the same intelligence that underlies Luke's account of the development of the Church in the Eastern Mediterranean, and the shift of the centre from Jerusalem to Rome, in Acts; it is the same intelligence that shows through in the apocalyptic visions of the triumph of the slaughtered lamb. I'm not of course suggesting that there are no differences between the authors of these different works. There clearly are, and these too are interesting in what they reveal of the way in which the authors worked out for themselves the significance of the crucified and risen Lord.

However, whatever the differences, the pivotal point around which all these writings revolve, is, with various degrees of explicitness, the risen victim; and the deep structure of their thinking is the intelligence of the victim.

Let me try now to show how the intelligence of the victim transformed the notion of the chosen people of Israel into that of the new Israel, and how it is that this brings us several steps closer to understanding how 'knowing Jesus' becomes a possibility for us. It is the story of how the intelligence of the victim went worldwide.

One of the things to which three of the gospels bear direct witness, Paul bears indirect witness, and John witnesses in another way, is that, on the night before he died Jesus celebrated a meal with his disciples, which he invested with a particular solemnity. All these witnesses show both that they, from their position as witnesses of the resurrection, understood that this celebration was a deliberate and climactic act on Jesus' part, and that Jesus understood this at the time. What Jesus did was not merely accidental, or full of significance only in the light of later events. It was full of a deliberate significance at the time, though only later events were to enable the other participants to begin to assess what that significance was. Again, it was the intelligence of the victim which was to make sense of that action, an intelligence that existed before the action in the life of the principal agent, Jesus, and after the action in the life of the others who were present. What it was that the crucified-and-risen Lord was able to illumine about that action is the subject of our exploration.

In the first place, it was significant that what was celebrated was a Passover meal. This was the celebration of the identity of Israel. It was the calling Israel out of Egypt, the bringing it to Sinai to receive the Law, and the movement towards, and entry into the promised land which constituted the self-understanding of Israel as the chosen people. Yet the Passover was the commemoration of an expulsion. By this stage the Egyptians wanted to expel the Israelites, who were seen as responsible for a whole series of disasters that had occurred in their land – the plagues which Moses produced. At the same time, Israel wanted to leave the heavy burden of slavery and go to live in freedom. So, we have a double dynamic: a movement towards freedom, given by God who heard the cry of his people, and decided to set them free, on the one hand; on the other hand, a movement to expel and destroy a hated group of foreigners with different customs, who were being roundly blamed for the serious disturbances within Egyptian society. So, the movement towards freedom and the movement towards an expulsion combine.

The original Passover supper is celebrated not after the escape from Egypt, but before it. It is the act which gives foundation to, and prior interpretation of, the flight. It is in this celebration that the identity of Israel is given. It shows that the identity of Israel is not simply the result of an expulsion, as a group which might be thrown together because of a particularly powerful experience, but which previously had nothing in common. Rather, Israel was chosen and given identity before the expulsion, so that God could establish a covenant with it. The freedom of election is prior to the experience of victimage. The meal interprets the flight which is to follow, and gives Israel a special understanding of itself as a victim people. The memory of its victimary status is constantly kept alive by the remembrance of the Passover.

This was, of course, only the beginnings of a project. It was God's project to build a quite new sort of society, a society that would be different from all the other societies. To this end God brought Israel out of Egypt, so as to establish with it a covenant by which the new sort of society would be built. It was to be different from the colonialism of Egypt, a slave-dependent society, different from the civic-feudal society of Canaan, different from the mercantilist societies of Phoenicia. Independence and equality were important. The laws of the covenant were to strengthen this self-understanding. It was to be a society where widows and orphans, exiles, sojourners, escaped slaves, would be able to live, that is to say, a society whose sense of values derived from its memory of slavery in Egypt, and its own escape from that society.

This new society had developed in its way of understanding how to live out its difference from other societies by means of various attempts to be faithful to God's project – for instance, through the monarchy. The experiment of the monarchy had failed, and the subsequent experience of the exile had taught other ways of trying to live the kingship of God, and fed developing hopes of a Messiah. What is important here is that in the time of Jesus (and indeed to some extent to this day), the way in which devout Jews understood the religion of Israel was not that it was a carefully disguised form of social control. Rather, it was understood as a movement, a search for fidelity to God's covenant, needing constantly to be kept alive, a movement to be different from other human societies. This movement involved a subversive understanding of the relationship of Israel to all other nations, of which a symptom was the feeling of superiority: Israel was not only different, but was showing the others up for what they were. To be faithful to God involves a constant conversion away from the idols of the nations to a pure observance of the commandments of God. Israel's roles as different, as superior, as bearer of the promises of God, and as victimary people were all interlinked. All these elements had, and have, their place in the celebration of the Passover.

Now, it is in the midst of this that Jesus comes and celebrates his Passover meal. Please notice that he didn't celebrate a sort of mock-Passover, or parody of the Passover with his disciples, so as to give them a different, critical basis for their relationship to Israel. He celebrated the Passover. That is, he inscribed his own understanding of what he was doing, and what God was doing, within the framework of the setting free of Israel, the victimary understanding of the chosen people, the giving of the covenant. It was not something done *instead* of the Jewish Passover. It was the Jewish Passover in its fulfilment: the Jewish Passover celebrated the night before his death by someone who knew that he was about to be murdered.

There is a great deal of Jewish material here that we may need reminding of, and which may seem excessively complicated to us, but which would have immediately rung all sorts of bells for Jesus' contemporaries. We may be tempted to think that all these allusions and echoes which we need to have explained to us, they also needed to have explained to them. Well, there was a lot that Jesus did need to explain to them, but to Jesus' contemporaries, much of this would have been assumed. For instance, when Jesus chose twelve disciples to be the leaders of his various followers, this had a specific set of resonances: twelve was the number of the tribes of Israel, and the choice of the twelve was a form of prophetic announcement that Israel was to be restored.

In the same way, the announcement, both by John, and by Jesus and his disciples, that 'The kingdom of heaven is at hand' or, 'The kingdom of God is at hand' would have struck its first hearers as saying something about the restoration of Israel, as the chosen vehicle of God's kingdom. The notion of God's kingdom would not have been heard as a vague term in which abstract qualities like justice and peace and mercy and faithfulness flourished; the automatic assumption would have been that it was very much bound to conceptions of the fulfilment of Israel, and its historical institutions. Even after the resurrection, the apostles ask Jesus, in Acts 1, 'Lord will you at this time restore the kingdom of Israel?'. It would be quite wrong for us to see Jesus as simply ditching Israel, and its hopes. He was subverting those hopes from within, operating from within the web of expectations that people had.

This can be seen from the way in which Jesus conducts his mission before going up to Jerusalem. He sets up a new trek, going across the sea of Galilee (rather than the Red Sea), and starting to feed the people, as Moses and Joshua had done on their way to the promised land. His teaching people about the scribes and Pharisees often carries the implication that they are Egyptians, from whom Israel must be set free. Here it is important not only that Jesus is revealing himself to be more than Moses, more than Elijah, more than Solomon, more than Jonah, more than Joshua, to name but the most significant of the Old Testament figures whose actions are recast and fulfilled by Jesus' own actions. It is important also that he is working out the whole framework of his mission within an understanding of God's relation with Israel. The Israel of God, which Jesus prepared and brought about was never intended simply as a break from Israel, but a subversion from within, so as to recast the meaning of Israel from within the categories the people of Israel already had.

I say all this since the last supper makes no sense

without a background understanding of what was being signified in the midst of what was already a highly symbolic meal. Just as the Passover meal interpreted the expulsion or flight from Egypt, so Jesus used the Passover meal to interpret his coming expulsion. Again, he made clear that he knew what was going on before the expulsion. There is present both the element of free self-giving, and the element of a victimary lynch. However it is the free self-giving that interprets the victimary lynch. Thus Jesus is able to talk about his blood poured out for many - borrowing the language of the suffering servant from Isaiah.

The Passover celebrated the flight from Egypt which led to Sinai, where Moses had made the covenant between the people of Israel and God. It was that covenant which established Israel as the people of God. The rite of the covenant (Exodus 24) involved the sprinkling of blood over the altar, and over the people. This was not, in all probability, a sacrifice for the expiation of sins, when it was first performed, but by Jesus' time it was understood as such. In Jesus' Passover supper, according to all the accounts we have (Matthew, Mark, Luke and Paul), Jesus used the language of covenant. He saw himself as establishing a new covenant in his own blood, in which he was both Moses and the oxen, both priest and victim. John has all this another way. John has Jesus being crucified a day earlier, at the time when the priests were slaughtering the Passover lambs in the temple, for the evening meal. He has the irony of the real sacrificial lamb being killed outside the city, and wearing a seamless tunic, the garment of the priest, on his way to Golgotha. So Jesus is the lamb, the priest, the temple and the victim all at once. John's deep and continual irony shows an entirely secular event - a semi-legal lynch death - as the real sacrifice which simultaneously shows up the nullity of religious sacrifice, and reveals the real basis by which humans maintain social order.

There are many further elements to Jesus' Passover, of which I'll deal with one in particular. All the accounts except Paul's have the element of the blood being poured out *for many* (*huper pollōn*). This is the use of the language of the suffering servant of Isaiah 53. Jesus is linking the Passover with the theme of vicarious expiation which is to be found in Isaiah. Traditionally, insofar as these passages of the Jewish Scripture were interpreted at all, it was to see Israel as the suffering servant, bearing the sins of the world. Jesus gives it a quite new meaning, since it becomes personal and messianic. Jesus then commands his disciples to do this in memory of him, thus giving this particular recasting of the Passover meal the same sort of function in the new Israel, the one Jesus was founding in his person, that the original Passover meal had had for Israel. It was to become the memorial feast whose celebration was to bring to memory, and thus make really present, the act of God which was being celebrated on behalf of his people.

The depth of Jesus' teaching and action is that he fulfils and subverts at the same time: the fulfilment is always subversive of, corrective of, the current practice. Now, I concentrate on this, the last supper, since it is how Jesus, before his death, interpreted his death. It was how he showed that he was giving himself freely, and yet being killed. It was how he shifted the meaning of the Passover, the covenant, the election of Israel, onto his person, such that the new Israel was to be a people who were founded in his lynch-expulsion just as the previous Israel was founded in their lynch-expulsion.

Please note that what I have been talking about, once again, is the intelligence of the victim. I have been talking of the way in which Jesus had a project for the refounding of the new Israel, which had to pass through his rejection, and where that rejection would in fact be the foundation for the new Israel. All this must have seemed deeply mysterious to the disciples, even as they shared the Passover celebration with Jesus. It was only after the resurrection, when they began to share the intelligence of the victim, that they began to see what it was all about. What they came to see was that the new Israel had been founded in those words, 'This is my blood of the covenant which is poured out for many'. The deliberate self-giving of Jesus into the hands of his murderers was, and had been understood to be by Jesus, a salvific act. It had made possible a new basis for humans to relate to each other.

I think it worth emphasizing something which, by the very familiarity of the words, we pass over without noticing. And that is: what an extraordinarily brilliant invention the last supper was. It was not something that just happened, and was understood later. Jesus was giving a unique, and brilliant nexus of teaching and interpretation of the Scriptures to his disciples in a mime, in acted-out form. It was the culmination of his teaching about the intelligence of the victim; it was the subtle recasting of the whole interpretative tradition to which Jesus was heir. I think we lose out if we think that, well, Jesus was God, so what he was doing he just did, and since he did it, and he was God, so we obey, and do it in memory of him. No, there was a profound human intelligence at work creating a radical new interpretation by the intelligence of the victim, showing, in a completely unexpected way, the hidden unity of God's self-revelation in those texts of Scripture. Jesus' last supper was not simply a mysterious divine disclosure, but was a divine disclosure exactly as a brilliant human interpretative invention.

Now, Jesus' celebration of the Passover is the interpretation he puts on his death. He sees it as a fulfilment of God's promises to Israel. Where before, Israel had been the victimary nation, attempting to build the kingship of God on earth, now it is Israel which victimizes the prophet who has come bringing out the full depth of God's revelation to Israel. That is to say, Jesus' death, at the same time as it is a fulfilment of God's deepest plan for Israel, the revealing of God as victim, is a critique of Israel's faith. What is shown is that Israel, like the other nations, builds its social structure on expulsion. It needs to expel in order to survive, like all other nations and social groups. That is to say, Jesus' interpretation of the Passover acts as a critique of Israel's infidelity to its calling as victimary people. In that sense, his interpretation of the Passover was the culmination of all his teaching, all of which tended to call back Israel to a deeper fidelity to God's promises and commandments, and which thereby acted as an intolerable critique.

Now, observe the subtlety and difficulty of what is being suggested here: two things are being claimed at the same time. It is being claimed that God gave Jesus to be the deepest fulfilment of his plan for Israel. The whole drift of the pattern of salvation that had been worked out in Egypt, the covenant, the monarchy, the exile, the Maccabean revolt, was slowly leading to the possibility of people understanding that God is the rejected one, God is the victim, God is amongst us as one we cast out. At the same time as this is being claimed, it is also being claimed that what made that revelation possible was the ignorance and blindness of the Jewish leaders. By rejecting the critique which Jesus made of their Judaism, and precisely in rejecting him, they exactly proved his point, and made the revelation possible of who God really was. So it is possible to say that Jesus' murder was a ghastly mistake, and yet that it was necessary. In various ways this phrase, 'it is necessary', 'it was necessary' comes up in different gospels. It is to this subtle confluence of intentions that the word refers. What had to be revealed was that all human societies, and not only all pagan societies, are based on deicide, the killing of God. For to be based on sacrifice, on killing, on casting out, is to be based on the exclusion of God, often enough under the

misapprehension that in excluding, you are serving
God.

What was revealed was quite different: the possibility
of a new and deeper Judaism. If Judaism was anyhow
far beyond all other social and cultural establishments
because of its victimary self-understanding and the
level of morality which sprang from that, the one further
step that could be made, and which needed to be made,
was the possibility of a Judaism where God was
worshipped *from* the victim, and not *over against*, or
by exclusion of, the victim. That is the difference to
Judaism that was made by the single act which
embraced the last supper and the crucifixion of Jesus.
Judaism was shown its deepest foundation.

From the moment, then, when the resurrection began
to make this clear to the disciples, there opened up the
possibility of living the new Israel of God. A new Israel
in the person of Jesus. The new Israel is not, please
notice once again, a simple departure from the old
Israel. What is radically new is new as a fulfilment of
something very ancient, and always threatens to lapse
into incomprehensibility unless its links with, and
critique of, the ancient covenant are constantly kept in
mind. What is offered is the possibility for humans to
form a new society which does not need victims or
exclusions in order for its sense of identity to be built
up. This is not because everyone is suddenly good, or
nice. Rather it is because the victim is given us: God
has provided for sacrifice. So, membership of this new
Israel involves a new way of relating to the victim. It
involves the unlearning of all those patterns of
behaviour which depend on, or tend to produce, victims,
of whatever sort. Simultaneously, it involves learning
how to relate to, side with, stand up for those who are
cast out, excluded and so on. It involves living for
others in such a way that those doing so are always
prepared to run the risk of expulsion and exclusion
themselves rather than basing their security on

expelling and excluding others. This is bearing witness to the truth which comes from the victim. The Greek word for witness is the word which gives us our word 'martyr'.

Let me emphasize once again that none of this could have begun to be understood apart from the resurrection of the crucified victim. The disciples on the road to Emmaus were leaving Jerusalem deep in disappointment, since the man they had thought would be the Messiah, the one to restore Israel, had been ignominiously put away. He had failed. With the resurrection comes the intelligence of the victim, comes the ability for the disciples to see quite suddenly what Jesus had been doing all along, and what a huge programme had been underway, not only in their lifetime, but in centuries long past. They were slow to see it, and its universal consequences, as we shall see. However, they now had the intelligence of the victim, and furthermore, they understood that whenever they met to obey the Lord's command to break bread and drink the cup in memory of him, that they had present with and among them the crucified-and-risen victim who was always the living foundation of the new Israel which they were constructing. The self-giving of Jesus, allowing him to be killed, which he had set forth by means of his Passover, was not restricted to that time and place alone. The resurrection gave back to the disciples that self-giving act of Jesus, so that from the time of the ascension onwards, the principal mode in which the crucified-and-risen Lord made himself present, and makes himself present to us, is in the making alive of his passover as the basis for the reconciliation of all humanity in a new society without victims.

The 'package', if you like, of the Passover makes the presence of the crucified-and-risen Lord not some accidental dip by God into our history. Rather it shows that that presence is part of an obscurely and astonishingly deep design running through thousands of years of history, whereby our humanity can be both fulfilled and rescued. The Last Supper was pivotal as Jesus' interpretation of what he was about, and pivotal, when the disciples began to understand Jesus' presence among them, with regards to the mission that they began to undertake.

We're now ready to go back to the first chapter, in which I attempted to set out something of the impact of the resurrection on the disciples. However, I hope we do so now with a fuller understanding of where the disciples were at when Jesus started to appear to them, and how their understanding was being shaped by the intelligence of the victim. With this background we can start to examine how this historically enriched intelligence of the victim led to the universality of the new Israel, and how it is this universality of the self-giving victim that is the basis for what is often called justification by faith. Luke and Paul will be our guides.

At the beginning of Acts, Luke tells the story of Pentecost. The story of the tongues of fire which came down and permitted the apostles to preach in all languages is not simply a description of what happened, it is at the same time the un-telling of another story, the story of Babel. That story, which occurs in Genesis 11, is about the human attempt to construct unity, and about how it led to chaos, separation, and breakdown of communication. Notice that the phenomenon of Babel is a pre-Jewish phenomenon. It is a story about how humanity, not just the people of Israel, came to be so divided. It is part of the pre-history of the chosen people, from before Abraham. God's choice of Abraham, and his founding of the chosen people was the beginning of God's reconstruction of a united human society, one that was not united in violence, and coercion; one that was not, in short, based on the murderous jealousy of Cain, or the arrogance of Babel.

This meant that God's choice of Abraham, and of Israel, was purely gratuitous. It was not because Israel was special that God chose it, but because God chose it that it was special. Through the ups and downs of its wavering adherence to its call, Israel came to an understanding of who God is that is quite outside the understanding of any nation, group or culture. By the knocks of their history, Israel was able slowly to move from the cult of a tribal deity, to that of a God above all other Gods, who is in special relationship with them, and reveals his law to them. Eventually, after the experience of the exile, and because of it, they move to an understanding that the God they worship is the only God; there is no other.

This is the story of the gradual purifying of the cult of God from idolatry, even the idolatry of the use of God to justify the superiority of 'our group' over anyone else's. In the prophets, who constantly criticized the idolatry implicit in the appropriation of God to national and military purposes, there are already signs of a universal approach to God. Isaiah proclaims that 'all the ends of the earth shall see the salvation of our God' (52.10). He has 'all nations' flowing to 'the mountain of the house of the Lord' (2.2).

The story of Jesus, is, as we have seen, in large part the story of how, when the time came for the next step in the purification from idolatry of Israel's worship of God, a large part of Israel was not prepared to accept the redefinition of their chosen-ness which this implied. They were not prepared to accept that it was not they, and their group boundaries which were special, but rather that it was God who is special, and is hidden by groups who try to make him their property.

What Jesus did was to challenge the way in which the Judaism of which he was a part maintained its unity over against others. So, for the Pharisees, goodness was clearly defined over against excluded others. The worship at the Temple separated Jews from Gentiles, rich from poor. Jesus sought, by his preaching and practice, to produce a new unity of Israel not based on exclusion or separation. This was why he went about preaching that 'the time is fulfilled, and the kingdom of God is at hand; repent and believe in the gospel'. However, the unity he managed to produce was in fact a unity against himself, in which he was cast out. It was necessary for one man to suffer so that the nation might not perish. In Caiaphas' words, spoken as priest and prophet, we have the unity and security of the nation assured by the exclusion of this man.

It was, as we have seen, Jesus' casting out that constituted the final and definitive purification of the Jewish religion. From then on, God, the utterly transcendent, the imageless, reveals that he can be the basis of no separative social or cultural unity at all. He can never be some sort of 'Gott mit uns' who backs up some group over against some other group. God revealed himself rather to be in between the violence of all groups; he revealed himself as the victim of all identities based on what I have called the 'over-against'.

Jesus revealed that the chosen people were still inclined, without knowing what they were doing, to base their cultural and religious unity on an exclusion. It was a chosenness that they had appropriated for themselves, rather than one conceived of as purely given. That which is purely given needs no over-against to define it. The sign in any of our lives that something is held as appropriated is exactly that it is defined or justified over-against some other group or person.

It is precisely this movement towards the revelation of the self-giving victim as the real basis of a new unity of a new Israel that underlies the two huge events which Luke describes in his vision of Pentecost, and his description of the baptism of Cornelius. The arrival of the Holy Spirit at Pentecost was the arrival of the presence of the crucified and risen Lord and the undoing of Babel. God's choice of Israel was already part of his reconstructing a reconciled humanity after the collapse of Babel. No longer, however, did God rely only on one people in order to reveal himself. Thanks to the preparation of the Jewish people, the victim at the base of all human societies had been revealed, and it was now possible to begin to build a new unity of the whole human race. All those, from whatever nation and tongue, who perceive the victim, who perceive their complicity in a society built on the making and hiding of victims, whose societies derive their identities over against some other group, all these can become part of the new Israel, the society built from the self-giving victim. This is the new Israel that is learning how to work its way out of being a victimizing society, and learning instead to live in imitation of and solidarity with the forgiving victim who is God. It is what Paul calls, at the end of his letter to the Galatians, the Israel of God.

Now what I am trying to convey here is something of the enormity of the change that was wrought in the understanding of the apostles, and in particular that of Peter, by the events of the resurrection. It is this that is attested by Luke. One of the first differences made by the presence of the crucified and risen Lord, a difference that took some time to sink in, was that Jesus' resurrection did not point to an internal reform of Judaism. It opened the way for Judaism to be turned into a universal religion. The revelation of God as the forgiving victim at the base of all human exclusions was the condition which made possible the construction of a society which did not define itself over against anything at all. Any society which does define itself over against anything at all cannot, by definition, be universal. It limits God to its own frontiers. For it to be possible to worship the true, non-tribal, non-partial, transcendent God who created and sustains everything, God had to reveal himself as the forgiving victim.

I hope now that some of the density of what is going on in the text of Acts comes alive. Little by little, the apostles realize that the risen Lord is the basis of a new,

universal, Israel. Babel is undone, and it becomes
possible for scattered humanity to become one new
people, people living from the risen and forgiving
victim. A completely unexpected discovery has been
made about how God relates to humanity, and not just
to Jews, such that it becomes necessary to announce
this novelty, this good novelty, to the nations. Again,
the power behind this movement is not some intellectual
think-tank. Peter and his colleagues would scarcely
make a very impressive think-tank. The power behind
this cultural cataclysm, if you like, was the presence of
the crucified and risen Lord, whose presence, and the
logic of whose presence pushed the fisherfolk and their
friends further afield than they could possibly have
thought up for themselves.

Luke bears witness to exactly this when, in chapter
10 of Acts he tells the story of the baptism of Cornelius.
This is the story of how Peter had to be pushed
unwillingly by God into participating in what is perhaps
the most significant date in the history of the world
outside Judaism, the date when Judaism went universal:
the first Gentile baptism. The presence of the crucified
and risen Lord started that process of breaking down
all cultural, racial, and national barriers that has been
the dynamic of its movement ever since.

Let me emphasize once again that if we look at
history in a simple linear fashion, we do not get the
sense of this movement. We look at a two-dimensional
process by which a movement started in Judaism and
moved outside it. Only the intelligence of the victim
makes apparent that there was nothing casual about
this. It was not just that a man rose from the dead, and
other men thought that everyone should know about
this, and so organized a series of international trips to
tell them. No. The man who died and rose again did so
as part of a process of making available to the whole of
humanity the possibility of forming a new human

society which maintains its unity in a completely different way from all human societies. That is, not by excluding, but by serving and worshipping, the victim. The mission to the Gentiles, the formation of the new Israel of God, is not accidental to the central fact of the resurrection, it is its direct implicate. The presence of the crucified and risen Lord to the disciples by his very existence was the foundation of the new Israel, and by the very dynamic of his presence as forgiving victim, spreads to all nations, unstoppably.

It can't be stopped because it is not a simply human feat. This is not to say that it grows because of some superficial divine magic. No, it grows because the presence of the forgiving victim is inescapably subversive of each and every human society that bases itself on victims, and on all and every human relationship that bases itself on exclusion. However obscurely people perceive this, they are still aware that a challenge is posed to their society, to their relationships. The voice of the victim, the voice of God, cannot be hushed.

This means of course that there is present in the group that lives from the forgiving victim, that builds its unity around the self-giving of Jesus, the beginnings of the possibility of a worldwide unity. A unity of all humanity, reconciled with each other, and, by definition, with God. So, the internal dynamic of the presence of the self-giving victim is always universal, always reaching further. This is because what is revealed is the dividing line which runs not between groups or classes of people, but within every human heart. The dividing line reveals whether or not I build my security and unity over against some victim, some excluded other, and thus depend on a separative, ever smaller sense of identity, or whether I am starting to receive my identity from the victim, and erect no barriers against the other, but find ever more common ground with the rest of humanity. When Vatican II talks of the Church as 'universal sacrament of salvation', it is to this that it is referring.

There is one further dimension to the presence of the crucified and risen Jesus I would like to bring out, and that is a dimension which cannot be separated from the dimension with which we have just been dealing. At the same time as the crucified and risen Lord is the foundation of the new Israel, so it is his crucified and risen presence that is the basis of the holiness of this new people. What is traditionally called 'justification by faith', is inseparable from the universality of the new community, or society, that the victim founds. There is no grace, or faith, that is not by that very fact immediately related to the new reconciled community. The new Israel is not tacked on to the making of humans holy, as an additional extra. Making us holy is identical with making us part of the new Israel of God.

Let me try and develop that. You will remember that what has been key throughout this book has been the intelligence of the victim. I have emphasized repeatedly that this involves a prior self-giving out of freedom. So, the whole process of Jesus' life was not simply the story of a lynch, but the story of a man who acted in freedom in certain ways which he knew would lead to his being killed. He did not want to be executed, but he knew he would be. He didn't allow that fact to change the way he acted or taught. And in fact what he taught was the same: he taught people how to act freely, how not to have their lives run by being locked, in an unhealthy or resentful way, into the life of someone else, or the life of the group that formed them. The symbol of this freedom is the ability to turn the other cheek, to go the second mile, and so on.

The importance of all that was the recognition that behind all of Jesus' life was a free self-giving, that was in no sense masochistic, in no sense contaminated by the violence of human relationships. Rather it was their antidote. It was this which, you remember, John saw as being the Father's giving of the Son, and the Son's obedience to the Father. That is, the free self-giving of Jesus, prior to any of the violence he underwent, was the divine hallmark of his mission. It was this element of self-giving that was totally gratuitous, not part of any human tit-for-tat or relationship of reciprocity, that was the witness to Jesus' being God.

Now, Jesus illustrated the depths of that free self-giving in his last supper. It was in the last supper that he gave a mimed definition of himself as the self-giving victim ('This is my blood of the covenant, which is poured out for many'). That is how Jesus was present among his disciples. It was that presence that was made alive again at the resurrection, when the crucified and risen Lord was the making alive of the self-giving victim as forgiveness for all victimizers. This means that when people talk about justification by grace through faith, the grace that is in question *is* the gratuity of the self-giving victim. There is no other grace. It is precisely that element of self-giving which was present in Jesus' life, up to and including his death, that is what is present to us as grace.

Now this has consequences! It means that holiness is our dependence on the forgiveness of the victim. That is to say, our being holy is dependent on the resurrection of the forgiving victim. And this, as we have seen, is exactly the same as the foundation of the new Israel, the beginnings of the new unity of humanity. The gratuity of the justification by grace through faith, and the gratuity which is the foundation of the new Israel is exactly the same gratuity. This means that justification by grace through faith automatically implies a relationship to the new Israel.

Let me try to say the same thing in a slightly different way, since this is a difficult concept to grasp for those of us brought up in an individualist society, and accustomed to an individualist account of holiness, or justification, or faith, or all three. The new unity of humanity, begun in the new Israel, has only this as its basis: that the resurrection has turned our victim into our forgiveness. Such as receive the forgiveness begin to form a new unity without any victims.

This means that what is given in Christ's victim death is a subversion of the old human way of belonging, and the possibility of our induction into a new human way of belonging, of being-with, without any over-against. This means that justification by faith belongs, in the first place, to the new community, the group receiving as a given its unity from the forgiving victim. It is exactly this making present of the beginnings of a new reconciled humanity which is the making present of justification by faith in the world.

There is, therefore, no such thing as individual justification by faith. Such a justification would imply a rescue of an individual from an impious world, over against which the individual is now 'good' or 'saved'. However, while the individual is still locked into some or other form of over-against, they are not yet receiving the purely gratuitous victim who has nullified all over-against. All justification by faith (that is, all faith) is a relational reality, flowing from, and tending towards the purely given unity of humanity in the victim. There is no grace that is not universal, that is not constantly creating and recreating the purely given unity of all humanity from the body of the victim.

Salvation, therefore, as it became present to the disciples at the resurrection, involved from the beginning a recasting of their way of relating to others, such that they were able to receive the purely given, without any appropriation to themselves of what was given as if it were somehow 'theirs'. We have already seen how Jesus' teaching was understood by the disciples in exactly this way. Part of the effect of the intelligence of the victim on their lives was their understanding Jesus' teaching on the importance, for instance, of forgiving so that we can be forgiven. It is the change in our relation with the other which permits and is permitted by the change in relation of God, the transcendent other, towards us. We are asked literally to loose, so that we may be loosed, to set free so that we may be set free – that is what the Greek word *aphiemi*, usually translated 'to forgive', means. Only in this way can our relationality be set free from the defensive self, which moves out of *ressentiment*, and enabled to become an interchange of gratuity.

I have already indicated how in the Sermon on the Mount, Jesus' teaching is about how freedom involves not being moved by any over-against, not being creatures of reaction. It is about our movement out of reaction, and into the receiving of the given that is simultaneously our movement into the purely given unity of humanity. The teaching is about how to relate to the social other as a gift, rather than a burden which defines and limits us. That which makes this movement possible is the forgiving victim, mediated to us in the transformation of human relationality. I ask you to think how different this sounds from the fairly standard view that lurks beneath not a few people's attitudes, an attitude which goes something like this:

In the Old Testament, religion was a collective thing, and as such, needed Law, and rites, and all that. However, Jesus came along, and preached a religion of grace, and the conversion of hearts, and this is an individual thing, not a collective one. So Christianity is essentially the religion of the free individual. If we were going to be radical, we'd have to get rid of rites, and any notion of church membership as anything other than voluntary association. However, for convenience sake we keep a lot of funny old rites, and ecclesiastical oddities, just so long as we remember that these are superfluous to what Christianity is really about.

I bring this up because it is by now, I hope, apparent that there is no change of heart that is not simultaneously a change in a way of belonging to a social other. And that of course means that there is no knowing Jesus outside the change of relationships that is the new Israel of God.

Now all this is an essential part of the package of the presence of the crucified and risen Jesus, which is what I'm trying to set out before exploring in detail ways in which we, at this distance, might genuinely know Jesus, the crucified and risen one. If it sounds complicated, it is in part because it is complicated. It is difficult for us to understand that the foundation of the new Israel is the same as the basis for all holiness, all justification, all conversion. We find it difficult to understand that justification by grace through faith is necessarily a collective phenomenon. It is collective because the only sort of salvation we have been given is the beginnings of the unity of the whole of humanity in a new society founded on the forgiveness of the risen victim. Grace is automatically collective: there is no grace that does not tend towards the construction of this new Israel of God. There is no faith in Jesus that is not intrinsically related to his founding and edifying this new humanity, and there is no making righteous that does not involve a movement away from a certain sort of social 'belonging', kept safe by casting out victims, and a simultaneous movement towards the fraternal construction of the people of the victim present in all the world.

Well, we're close to the end of what looks like a long introduction to the subject of 'knowing Jesus'. We can't begin to talk about knowing Jesus without setting out pretty clearly the circumstances in which he gave himself to be known, the purpose of his project. We can't begin to relate to him, that is, except in the light of, and as part of all that. To do otherwise would be to run an even greater risk of constructing a relationship with Jesus in our own image.

I have therefore been setting out the parameters of what there is to be known in knowing Jesus by filling out the density of the apostolic witness - what it is that the apostles witness to when they give witness to the resurrection of Jesus. I have tried to show how it was that the presence of the crucified and risen Lord is the foundation of the new Israel, is the source of all conversion, and grace, all holiness and forgiveness, and how this is a universal phenomenon. I have, in short, tried to show that to say 'I believe in the resurrection' directly implies also saying, 'I believe in the Church which is one, holy, catholic and apostolic'.

That is to say, the new Israel which Jesus founded in his death and resurrection, a real community of people which foreshadows the reconciliation of humanity with God, is one, because it has the unique foundation of the unique self-giving victim; it is holy because this community is founded entirely on the forgiveness of this victim; it is catholic because, at the same time as being one, it is also universal, knowing no bounds of culture, or race, or language, because it is not founded over against anything at all, but purely given; and it is apostolic, because what is kept alive by the Holy Spirit is the presence of the crucified and risen Lord as witnessed to by the apostles. What is handed on through the centuries is the apostolic witness which is the guiding norm of all assessment of what does or does not constitute the Christian faith.

The principle way by which all this is kept alive in our midst is: the eucharist. Everything that I have said so far about the presence of the crucified and risen Lord can legitimately be taken as referring to the Mass. The real presence of Jesus in the eucharist is the real presence of the crucified and risen Lord, giving himself, founding the new Israel, making possible the conversion of those who participate. It is the real presence of the grace which justifies. In all the other celebrations which we call sacraments, one or other dimension of this presence of the crucified and risen Lord is emphasized. In the eucharist however, the whole package is present, if only we have open eyes and hearts to perceive it, and to receive him!

So I have set out the framework within which any talk of knowing Jesus, and not only any talk, but also any real knowledge of him, makes sense, and is not suspect of delusion. In the final chapter I will attempt to fulfil the promise of the title of this book.

Questions

1. What did Jesus think of himself as 'founding' or bringing about when he talked of the Kingdom of God? How do we know this? How did Jesus both use and at the same time subvert Jewish institutions and practices as part of his teaching and activity?

2. How did Jesus use the Passover to interpret his own forthcoming death, and what does this tell us about the possibility of building a universal Judaism? Is 'Universal Judaism' an appropriate way for us to talk about Christianity?

3. What does it mean to say that, starting from Jesus' self-giving up to death, we are to worship God *from* the victim rather than *over against* a victim? How does this teach us to be alert to our own capacity for creating victims, thinking that in doing so we are serving God?

4. When you join with other Christians to celebrate Mass, the Eucharist, or the Lord's

Supper, is this a gathering of penitent stone-throwers listening to the crucified and risen victim explaining scriptures and being enabled to imagine new, victimless ways of building each other up in fraternity? If it is not this, what is it, and why?

5. What does it mean to say you are justified by faith? How do you receive holiness from a group of those in the process of discovering their forgiveness? What might it mean to discover that you don't have to justify yourself to anyone at all, and are loved just as you are? What might it mean for your group not to need any 'enemies', 'outsiders' or 'impure people' over against whom to define your goodness? How might this help your construction of community?

4
A Framework of Knowing

In a sense, I rather hope that this chapter might be unnecessary, for much of what I'll be doing is trying to draw out what I hope has become apparent from the previous chapters with relation to knowing Jesus, and just focusing it a little. What I hope I have conveyed is how the crucified and risen Jesus made himself known to his disciples, and consequently, through their witness, to us. Let me try and work back, therefore from where I ended in the last chapter, to where I started in the first, looking at each dimension which the risen Lord makes present and alive, so as to see how each one will bring us a little closer to knowing Jesus.

We ended with the presence of the universal victim as the foundation for a new unity of humanity. I think therefore that one of the first questions we can ask ourselves about whether or not we know Jesus is: to what extent are we caught up in a sectarian frame of mind? To what extent are our responses tribal? Let me suggest ways in which we might be: whenever we behave as though some group to which we belong is self-evidently superior to, more truth-bearing than, some other group. That is to say, whenever there is a note of comparison in our reactions and behaviour. The comparison can be to our favour, as when we consider ourselves superior, or to our detriment, as when we take on the role of the oppressed victim of society, or whatever. Both of these comparative forms of behaviour betray that we have not found the givenness of the self-giving victim as the foundation of our unity.

So, for instance, Catholics may easily talk of Protestants, or Muslims, as though the Catholic Church were superior to these other groups. Thus, belonging to the Catholic Church makes of one a superior sort of person: after all one knows the truths of the faith, and belongs to the true Church. This attitude is not uncommon, and it gives a sort of feeling of combative brotherhood with other fellow Catholics, a strengthened sense of belonging as one faces up to a world run by a hideous army of Protestants, pagans, Masons and what-have-you. In some countries the word 'Jew' would traditionally be part of this list of others. Well, I hope that gives it away. The unity that is created in this way – even the laughing emotional bonding that seems to have no practical consequences, is created at the expense of a victim or victims, at the expense of an exclusion. That is to say, it is a unity that is derived over-against some other. And that is to betray the very deepest truth of the Catholic faith, the universal faith, which by its very nature, has no over-against. The unity which is given by and in the risen victim is purely given. It is indicative of no superiority at all over anyone else. Anyone who genuinely knows the crucified and risen victim can never again belong wholeheartedly to any other social, or cultural, or religious group. He or she will always belong critically to all other groups, because all other groups derive their unity over-against someone or some other group.

The only unity to which he or she cannot escape belonging is the new unity of humanity that the Holy Spirit creates out of the risen victim, the unity which subverts all other unities. And this new unity, given us in the Catholic Church is not yet a realized unity, as must be apparent. The Church does not teach that it is the kingdom of heaven, which is the realization of the unity in the new Israel, but that it is the universal sacrament of that kingdom. That is to say that it is the efficacious sign of a reality that has been realized only in embryo. As such, it is radically subversive of all other forms of belonging, all other ways of constructing unity. But it is so as a gift from God.

So, knowing Jesus implies, of necessity, a gradual setting free from any tribal sense of belonging, and the difficult passage into a sense of belonging that is purely given. Its only security is the gratuity of the giver, and that means a belonging in a group that has no 'abiding city', that unlike the fox, has no hole, and unlike the bird, has no nest. You can see, I think, why it is particularly sad when Catholics turn belonging to the Church into a sectarian belonging, into a definable cultural group with a clearly marked inside and outside, and firm ideas as to who belongs outside. Of such people it can be said that they do not go in to the kingdom of heaven, and throw away the key so that others may not enter. By their very sectarian insistence on the unique truth of Catholicism, these people cut themselves off from access to the truth which they think is theirs, but which is only true when it is received as given.

The flip side of this sign of knowing or not knowing Jesus is the adoption of the role of victim, one of the key moves in modern society if you want to establish your credentials, and make space so as to be tolerated. I imagine that almost all of us at one time or other have felt the pull of this cultural imperative: if we can cast ourselves as victims, then this makes us pure and innocent. Society is the villain. This is a tactic for any number of so-called 'minority' groups in society, and for any number of individuals in their relationships. It is a way, too, of covering up my violence, or the violence of the minority group, by blaming the (usually nebulous) other for all my ills. It can thus be a potent form of emotional blackmail, as well as making it very difficult to distinguish cases where people really are being persecuted, and something must be done about it, from cases where people are using their sacred status as

victims to get away with what no other person or group
would be able to. I am sure that all of you can think of
examples of this mechanism in operation from your
own history.

Now, again, the knowledge of Jesus, the crucified
and risen victim makes a difference here. For if you
know the crucified and risen victim, you know that you
are not yourself the victim. The danger is much more
that you are either actively, or by omission, or both, a
victimizer. We only have one self-giving victim, whose
self-giving was quite outside any contamination of
human violence or exploitation. The rest of us are all
involved with that violence. The person who thinks of
him or herself as the victim is quick to divide the world
into 'we' and 'they'. In the knowledge of the risen
victim there is only a 'we', because we no longer need to
define ourselves over against anyone at all.

So, knowing the universal victim involves a conversion
in these very deep areas of our belonging and our way
of relating. Any talk of knowing Jesus that permits the
sectarian attitude, the 'we'/'they', might well give cause
for suspicion. You can see once again how the theme of
the universality of the victim, and hence of the Church,
and the theme of justification by faith, are the same
theme in the light of this. For the whole point of
justification by faith is that it is justification by God,
not self-justification. The whole problem Luther had
with works was that he took the Catholic insistence on
good works to be necessarily a source of self-justification.
Self-justification is of course when I justify myself over
against someone, or something else. I am trapped in a
defensive, or self-justifying position if I constantly
depend on comparison with, or approval from, others.
That means that my sense of identity, my security is
built over-against others, and is not simply, gratuitously
given. I am dependent on various ways of showing that
I am different, separate, not part of the crude mass of
humanity. Self-justification and the sectarian attitude

are exactly the same phenomenon. The given-ness of goodness by God, implying the growing appreciation of my similarity to, and my lovability as one of, the crude mass of humanity which is loved by God; the givenness of justification, and the givenness of the universality, the catholicity, of salvation, are one and the same phenomenon. In this way the individual and the group simultaneously learn to live without any over-against, defining themselves against no one at all. That is a sure sign of a real knowledge of Jesus.

Let us briefly go a stage further back. Knowing Jesus is inseparable from knowing Jesus in the eucharist. I tried to indicate how Jesus had concentrated his self-giving in the sign which he gave his disciples at the last supper. In the celebration of this sign, the Holy Spirit makes present the whole self-giving of God to us as man. It is exactly as self-giving, crucified-and-risen Lord that Jesus is present in this sacrifice. It is the only real sacrifice because it is the celebration of the self-giving of God into the hands of murderous men, and not the giving by murderous men of something or someone to God which or who might cover up their guilt.

Now there are of course people who have been scandalized, that is, caused to stumble, by false teaching over the centuries regarding the presence of Jesus in the Mass. I do not say that because they do not know that the crucified and risen Lord is truly present as such in the Mass, thus they do not know Jesus. The problem is with those who caused them to stumble. However, it is wrong to imagine that a real knowledge of Jesus can coexist for long with a complete ignorance of his own interpretation of his self-giving, which showed the pattern of his whole life, and showed clearly the nature of the sort of new Israel he was bringing into being. Certainly, for someone who has received the completely unmerited privilege of the gift of the Catholic faith, the eucharist is pivotal for knowing

Jesus. It is, if you like, the ordinary, regular way in which we know Jesus. Any visions, or feelings that someone might have, may or may not be useful or profitable to that person, as the case may be. A certain criterion, however, is that if these visions or feelings lead their recipient to play down, or despise, the ordinary way in which the crucified and risen Lord makes himself present to the people he seeks to bring into the new Israel, then there is something wrong.

For the presence of the crucified and risen Lord in the eucharist is how Jesus gave himself to be known: as one without form or beauty, as one who serves, as one who gives himself for the life of the world. Any knowledge which contradicts that is not the knowledge of Jesus. Now, please note how, as you would expect, the themes of the universality of the victim, and justification as flowing from, and depending on, the self-giving of the victim, are automatically present in this celebration, which is simultaneously the making and keeping alive of the founding of the new Israel, and the making present to all the faithful of the one whose forgiveness makes them just.

Because it is the celebration of the presence of the crucified and risen Lord whose resurrection is our forgiveness, it is also the place of our conversion. I wonder whether there is any deeper conversion than the slow, almost imperceptible change wrought in us by the crucified and risen one, whereby we cease to think of ourselves primarily as victims, and start to see ourselves primarily as actual, or potential persecutors. Of course, this change of heart can only take place in the midst of real community situations and relationships, probably amidst real conflict. This is the sort of healing that goes right to the centre of our lives, our fantasies, our projections, our paranoia, our insecurity. For to be able to be a penitent persecutor, or a penitent traitor – to be able to be Paul or Peter – is not something that comes at once. The forgiveness may come to us first as the healing of our weakness, our self-pity, our sense of being awful, so that little by little we may have the strength, and dignity, and freedom to be able to be aware of ourselves not as sinned against, but as sinning. The extraordinary virility of soul that it takes to be able to stand free and see the other, the community, the group, not in defensive terms, not as a 'they', but as a we, and a we in which I may be a stumbling block rather than a building block, that is part of the healing mystery of the Mass.

This conversion, the possibility of which is constantly made present to us by the presence of the crucified and risen victim, is not just an individual thing. It involves the recasting of our solidarity, such that we cease to share in the ways of relating to the other, the group, which rely on exclusion, and start instead to undergo the transformation of our sense of being. This is worked out by a new form of solidarity, a new way of belonging that does not depend on exclusion, and where we live with some fear that we may be excluders, where we learn to create the unity that does not depend on casting out. At any given celebration of the eucharist, that is the dynamic of what is going on, the conversion that is being made present. It is the Catholic faith that not even a grossly sinful priest, not even a grossly obtrusive liturgy (whether by its too little, or its too much, pomp and dignity) can overcome the presence of the risen Lord who is working this change in his people.

I should, I'm quite sure, add a footnote to this, with respect to the presence of Jesus in the reserved sacrament. For those who are not Catholics, I had better explain: this is the custom of keeping consecrated hosts in a tabernacle in a visible position in a church or chapel, with a perpetual flame, often red, burning before it to indicate that the Blessed Sacrament is present. It is the custom of Catholics to genuflect each time they pass the tabernacle. Processions carrying the sacrament are sometimes organized, as well as services of adoration of, and blessing with, the Blessed Sacrament, known as Benediction. For many Catholics, as well, the privileged place of prayer *par excellence* is before the Blessed Sacrament, because it is a rich sign of Jesus' presence. The point of this footnote is merely to indicate that the presence of Jesus in the reserved sacrament is, of course, the same presence as in the Mass. That is to say, the presence is, as always, that of the crucified and risen Jesus made present as our forgiveness, and prayer in the presence of the risen Lord is therefore able to enmesh the person praying into the various deep changes that are made available by the resurrection. It is perhaps one of the most privileged ways of working out in quiet and solitude the change of relationships which must be worked out as well in concrete ways in the context of daily life.

Let us look, then, at how it is that the crucified and risen victim made present to us is able to affect forgiveness in our lives. Key here, I think, is the role played by our memories. Forgiveness and memory are intrinsically linked. What is referred to as the healing of memories and the forgiveness of sins, are part of the same package. Normally the sort of memories that need healing are the effects of other people's sins or omissions on our life, and the sins that need forgiving are the ways, also present as memories, in which we have dealt destructively or manipulatively with others, perhaps even treating ourselves as a sort of 'other' whom we destroy and manipulate. What these forms of behaviour have in common is that the way in which we are tied in with others is distorted. At many different levels we are locked in various forms of defence, aggression, rivalry, and so on, with other individuals, and indeed with others as a whole. We can tell that it is not just other individuals that are in question when we become aware of the ways in which we indulge in repetitive mechanisms, playing out the same distorted rituals and patterns of behaviour against quite other people than we regarded as responsible for them.

Now, in our relations with the social other which forms us we can make a basic mistake. We can assume that what we think, how we feel, is original to us. We are unique, and our little independence needs protecting over against that social other. This means being locked into an attitude of resentment towards the other, blaming it for our ills, and becoming ever more convinced that we are not only right, but special, a kind of lonely hero, or victim in the midst of an unjust world. Here I am not talking about cool ratiocination, but about the attitudinal patterns of the heart which surface in our behaviour, without us being fully aware of them.

Part of the problem here is that we assert our independence of, and deny our dependence on, the social other which surrounds us. The trouble with this is that it locks us into an inability to change. Because the truth is that we are not independent of the social other. Perhaps especially the person who is most convinced of his or her independence is locked into the other, which he or she desperately needs as a sounding board, or counter example, by comparison with which to demonstrate his or her own excellence. The truth is that we are completely dependent on the social other. Not only did it give us birth, and does it give us food and so on, the obvious things which existed before we came along, and which we receive as part of a long history, but it gives us language, thought patterns, and even desires. In all these things we are preceded by, and formed by a social other. Our learning to imitate these things is our induction into being humans.

The problem is that the social other which forms us is, and was before we came along, a violent other, full of the distortions, cruelty, murder and exploitation which abound all over the planet. That is to say, along with the way in which it brings us into being human, which

is a good thing, there are introduced at the same time
all sorts of violences and disturbances. Each of us is
locked into the social other in a series of vicious circles.
That we can perceive this at all is thanks only to the
presence of the crucified and risen Jesus. There would
be no way for us even to perceive fully the violence of
the other which forms us unless there were something
different, if you like, a different sort of other, which is
not part of the violent other which forms us.

That is precisely what is made present by the
gratuitously self-giving victim. You may remember how
early on in this book, I stressed the way in which the
self-giving of Jesus to his death, and the giving of him
back in the resurrection, were entirely gratuitous. They
were absolutely outside the tit-for-tat and reciprocity of
the 'world'. However, they were not only motiveless
acts of generosity. What was given was something
revealing the human condition, revealing the basis of
the violence by which we are locked into each other. It
took God to allow us to kill him, for him to be able to
loose us from the deepest ways in which we are locked
into the violent social other. Only forgiving us for that
would really forgive us. Again, the word 'forgive' means
'to loose': only to loose us from that would really loose
us.

The level at which the presence of the crucified and
risen Jesus thus makes impact on our lives is precisely
at the level of our identities being formed in distorted
relationship with the social other. A different social
other, if you like, breaks into the way in which we are
tied in, permitting us to be loosed, and to have our
identity, our dependence on a new, pacific, other, re-
formed. So, it is the irruption of this completely new,
peaceful other into our pattern of relating that is able to
let us loose exactly insofar as we let others loose. This is
emphasized by Jesus in parable after parable and
teaching after teaching: God forgiving us, and our

forgiving others, are parts of the same act. There is no forgiveness of one without forgiveness of the other.

Now, in the case of all of us, this means that our whole relationship with what is other than us changes, and can be felt, however slowly, to change. We are able to loose those memories which bound us in to places, circumstances or relationships, leaving us feeling powerless and oppressed by them. We are enabled to perceive how what we have done, and what we have justified to ourselves, has partaken of the same destructive relationship with the other, and repent of it.

Let's look more closely at what an act of repentance is: it involves seeing the discrepancy between a relational pattern of violence, and the new, pacific relational pattern that has been made present by the forgiving victim, and seeing how we have been dependent on the violent pattern, while we thought we were being free. The realization of our dependence is the beginning of our healing and forgiveness, for that means we are already starting to relate pacifically to what is other than us. The clean sorrow which this realization produces in us, and the beginnings of the adopting of new patterns of behaviour is what constitutes our forgiveness, for it is what constitutes our new heart, our change of mind – metanoia – the deep change in our attitudinal patterns towards patterns of peace with relation to the other. Catholics have the incomparable privilege of having this whole process made obvious and simple in the confessional, where the priest acts as an efficacious sign of the deep forgiveness that is being fed them by the crucified and risen Lord.

Because of the gratuity of his presence, the crucified and risen Lord works at undoing the ways in which our memories and our violences lock us into what is other than us. At the very deepest level of our being, therefore, the level which makes consciousness possible, the level which the Hebrews referred to as 'the heart', there is no knowing Jesus, the crucified and risen Lord, without the possibly slow, possibly dramatic, upheavals in the patterns of our relating which I have been trying to describe.

Precisely as part of knowing Jesus, we can expect the upheaval that will take us out of being the lonely hero, denying dependence on a rotten and corrupt world, into being terribly ordinary. One of the guarantees of knowing Jesus is that a person has become steadily more at home with being part of rotten and corrupt humanity. He or she is steadily more aware of his or her complicity in its faults and violences, and doesn't seek to hide that. They know that it is as part of the human mass that they are able to be touched by the new sort of dependence on the new sort of other which is coming into the world as a forgiving victim. So, our memories, rather than blocking us off from others, are made healthy by plugging us in with others, but in new ways; our sins however vile, rather than becoming a motive of separation, are turned into the beginnings of a new sort of solidarity – and if you doubt that, look at any group of Alcoholics Anonymous. We even learn to hate our sins not as part of the self-hatred that no amount of apparent worldly success can cover up, but because of the effect they have on others. That is: the whole of our relationality is re-cast.

It would not be enough to see the risen-crucified one merely setting us free to 'belong' to the world. There is more than that. Our desires that were formed in violence are transformed not by magic, but by a new sort of practical learning, which like all our learning works by imitation. We learn to imitate the self-giving victim, drawn on by the intelligence of the victim which both sets us free to act gratuitously, reveals to us our and other people's outcasts, the inconvenient ones, and empowers us to works of service, of solidarity with them and so on. By concrete, practical acts of relearning, which will at first strain against our old attitudinal patterns, we acquire new desires, and our whole person is formed by new desires, in imitation of the one in whose desires, in whose imitation, there are no stumbling blocks, no rivalry. The other which forms us ceases to be the world with its violent, rivalistic desires, by which we cause each other scandal, cause each other to stumble. Rather the other which forms us becomes the spirit of the self-giving victim. We become possessed by the crucified and risen one, by a slow process of entrancement, or possession, which has to pass through concrete acts of increasing freedom and service. That, I think, is what Paul meant when he said: 'It is no longer I who live, but Christ who lives in me' (Gal. 2.20). He was talking about the pacific possession, which is the reforming of the whole of the person that is constituted by desire. He was talking about the fruition of the process constituted by progressive acts of imitation of the self-giving one, inspired by the intelligence of the victim. The concrete acts, the works of imitation, are exactly the way grace makes available to us the freedom which is possession by Christ.

This is part of the package of knowing Jesus, being affected in this sort of way. If someone says that they know Jesus, and this is not a part of what they are talking about, then I would be suspicious. Please note again, that what I am referring to, the Jesus who is known, the only Jesus that there is available to be known, is the crucified and risen victim. Simultaneously his presence works this deep transformation of forgiveness, and introduces us into the universal new Israel. These are not even separate acts: our forgiveness, our healing, our conversion, the development of the new heart by concrete works of service and self-giving, the new patterns of relating, the dropping the need for self-justification, for identity by comparison, and the being inducted into the new Israel of God, the Catholic Church; all this is the same thing.

Just as I have insisted that people who say they

know Jesus, but don't know, or have no perception of these things, may well be fooling themselves, so I think it important to say that the many people who would be nervous of saying that they know Jesus, and yet *do* know these things, *are* aware of them as part of a slow, perhaps uneven experience, may well be fooling *them*selves. For to know these things is indeed to know the power and presence of the crucified and risen Jesus.

So far I have attempted to set out ways by which we can make sense of talk of 'knowing Jesus', derived from what we have gleaned about the Jesus who is to be known. Now I propose to be a bit less indirect in my approach, by looking at some existing models of knowing Jesus, and comparing them with what Jesus himself has to say about such things from the gospel of John.

Throughout this book I have been trying to emphasize that talk of knowing Jesus has its proper place in the language of the faith. I've been trying to indicate all sorts of ways of knowing, of awareness and perception, which might not strike you straight away as to do with 'knowing'. What I'd like to do is to take the sort of knowing that I've been discussing, a knowing that has objective, public consequences, and that produces changes in relationship over time and over a whole range of feelings, and to compare that with some ways of talking which suggest that knowing Jesus is like knowing a secret friend.

You are probably aware as I am of the existence of what one might call an 'intimist' spirituality - I've borrowed the word from Spanish - 'intimista'. It is a way of being 'spiritual' that is greatly to do with personal feelings. Now, in this way of thinking, knowing Jesus might be a strong personal experience that can't really be explained to other people. It might be a sudden intensification of religious feeling that seems to make a unitary sense of that person's life. There are any number of possible experiences of this sort that might be thought by the one experiencing them to be experiences of knowing Jesus.

Now, from what I have been saying thus far, you can probably guess where I'm going here. Does the recipient of the experience consider him or herself to have been set apart from others by it? Because, if they do, then one wonders how this can be an experience of the crucified and risen Lord. An experience of the crucified and risen Lord brings a person to be more, not less, common, more not less inclined to love the human race, and acknowledge his or her dependence on it. It inclines a person to be less inclined to judge and to consider themselves separate from others. The reason I stress this, is because there are some teachings around which make a certain sort of experience the criterion for being a real Christian. The experience is made into a real divider, a stumbling block.

This has nefarious consequences. One is that the person in question thinks that they have 'made it'. They are 'saved', or whatever the language they care to use is. That is a terrible mistake, because they have made of a single, or a series, of experiences, a substitute for a relationship, working over a long period of time, inducing profound changes in that person's life. The only way to test out the health of the relationship is to look not at feelings, but at the patterns of relating with concrete others, and particularly with the sort of concrete others with whom Jesus identified himself – the poor, the naked, the imprisoned, the sick, and on and on. A private experience, called 'knowing Jesus' can never be a substitute for a public change in ways of relating, within the public framework by which Jesus makes himself to be known – the sacraments, and victims. The person who really thinks that a private experience of knowing Jesus is what will stand him or her in good stead at the last judgement must prepare for the shock that on that day the one whom they claim to have known may turn to them and say, 'I tell you, I do not know you'. There's nothing subjective about the criteria set out in Matthew 25, the parable of the sheep and the goats.

The second nefarious consequence is on the person who doesn't have such an experience, but is yet a believer, perhaps a believer who has great difficulties in whole areas of his or her life. For this person, the insistence on an intimate experience of knowing Jesus can be a crushing burden. It can further and deepen this person's sense that they are not really lovable, and they're not really up to it as a Christian. Other people seem to have this marvellous experience, and talk radiantly about Jesus, or speak in tongues, or whatever, but this person stumbles along feeling somehow left out by God.

Well, of course, it's a lie that that person is left out by God, and it's certainly true that God longs for that person to be able to love him or herself, to have a higher self-esteem, so as better to be able to love others. It may indeed be true that genuine, and wonderful feelings are in store for that person. But they'll never find that out while they're caused to stumble by the insistence on certain sorts of feeling. Rather, they'll continue to be locked into a certain sort of jealousy whereby they either see themselves as, or are made to feel, second-class Christians, by comparison with the ones who've had the experience. Now, there's only one way out of that, which is by stepping outside the whole field of tension surrounding personal experiences, learning to stop comparing themselves with others, and relaxing instead into the public ways in which the crucified and risen Jesus makes himself present, and shows them his love. They will have to learn how to renounce the desire for experience or experiences, as they discover that those very desires, spiritual-seeming as they are, are riddled with envy and rivalry. It is towards helping that happen that this book has been aimed.

It is worth pointing out here how, in the history of

the Church, so many of the saints (but not all!) have been deeply reticent about their personal experiences of Jesus. This is not to say that they haven't had them, but the very hallmark of their being genuine was that their recipients had a horror of publicity. The key reason for this was twofold: they had a deep sense of the ease with which they could deceive themselves; and they did not want whatever they might have experienced to be a stumbling block - a motive for jealousy or rivalry - among those who did not have such experiences. In short, they did not want to scandalize others. That desire, to help others avoid stumbling blocks, is about as clear an indication as could be had that a real knowledge of Jesus is at work, for the making possible of discipleship in others is precisely teaching imitation without rivalry as Jesus taught it.

The third nefarious consequence of any great insistence on personal experiences in knowing Jesus is that this ends up constituting a barrier to faith for non-believers. If what they hear is a great deal of talk of personal experiences, with the suggestion, or affirmation, that without such an experience you're not really 'in', then what better excuse is there for not bothering about taking the faith seriously. I might think as follows: 'If there were a God, and he wanted me to take him seriously, then he would give me one of these experiences, which would make me a Christian, and I would take him seriously. Since he hasn't given me one of these experiences, I needn't bother about religion'. Well, this is nonsense. God has made himself publicly known more or less everywhere, by this stage of the twentieth century, in the person of a publicly executed victim. The revelation of the forgiving victim is publicly available more or less everywhere on the face of the planet, and faith comes by this revelation being preached by those for whom it has become something to which they can give witness.

Now, please don't let me give you the impression

that I'm against personal experiences of the love of God, or knowing Jesus. Far from it. But these will happen to whom they will happen, and are in no sense a criterion for anything at all. Even those who have them may do better to ignore them, on the traditional grounds that one small work of charity is of more value before God than the highest degree of mystical ecstasy. Those who don't have them should certainly ignore them, on the grounds that no desire that is fuelled by jealousy can be of God. How can God give us what he wants for us, if we are so determined to have the same sort of feeling as we hear that X or Y has? The problem with jealousy is that it involves desiring something in imitation of someone else, when what someone else has doesn't suit us; but we can't receive what does suit us because we are too caught up in the imitation of the other.

No private experience of Jesus as one's friend, as one's mate, as someone you talk to across the room, is any substitute for the much more radical knowledge of Jesus which I have been trying to put before you, and whose effect on a person's life is a slow, but massive empowerment of the whole of that person's life. They are empowered to break free from a series of ways of relating, and deepen into other ways of relating whose consequences may indeed be felt in their own lives, but more strikingly, could be perceived and described by any onlooker, and would clearly involve a turning towards the victim.

Now, when I use a phrase like, 'a slow but massive empowerment of the whole of a person's life', I am not making this up. There is a passage in John 14 (verses 22–24) in which Judas (not the Iscariot) asks Jesus, 'Lord how is it that you will manifest yourself to us and not to the world?'. Jesus replies: 'If a man loves me, he will keep my word, and my Father will love him, and we will come to him, and make our home with him'. Now this seems at first a very odd answer to the question,

'How will you manifest yourself to us?'. It is odd because it does not talk about a manifestation *to* anyone at all, in terms of an appearance outside you or me, by which we might know or see or recognize the one appearing. The manifestation is within the life and relational patterns of the person.

John's terminology is different from the one I use, but the phrase 'keep my word', just like the phrase 'keep my commandments', covers the area of loving imitation, as is shown in the giving of the new commandment: love each other even as I have loved you. The element of imitation is inscribed forever in the commandment to love. So, when Jesus replies to Judas, 'If a man loves me, he will keep my word, and my Father will love him, and we will come to him', he is not talking about some Kantian straining of the will, but of an imitative pattern by which the person becomes possessed by the other: 'We will come to him and make our home with him'. By keeping the word, imitating the love, we allow ourselves to be possessed. And that is how Jesus is made manifest to us and not to the world: by ourselves being made into signs of his possession of us. That is exactly the whole empowerment of a person's life to which I referred. It means that Jesus is not 'other' to us, as a bad conscience is 'other' to us, a representative of some force that's bullying us. Jesus is other to us as God is other to us, able to move us entirely from within our freedom without displacing it. If you want 'evidence' for Jesus being God, that is it, and John offers just this as evidence that Jesus is God when he quotes Jesus as saying, 'In that day you will know that I am in the Father, and you in me, and I in you' (14.20). Jesus makes himself known as God by turning us into other Christs at the level at which only God can change us.

Now, in what is positively the last section of this book, let me turn to one slightly surprising suggestion, caused by looking at John's gospel. The suggestion is this: that Jesus is really not at all interested in people knowing him.

Let me explain. There is no sense in which Jesus is an end in himself. And this is part of the presence of the one who frees us from stumbling blocks. Supposing you want to go to a concert, and before the concert starts, someone comes on stage and gives an explanation of what is going to happen, so that you will appreciate it better. Well, that's fine insofar as the announcer comes on quickly, does his or her bit, and gets off again. However, you've probably been to occasions when the announcer seems to have misunderstood his role. He seems to think that the public actually wants to listen to him, is amused by him, regards him as of some importance. This is embarrassing, because what is revealed is the man's self-importance, quite out of proportion to his real role as a signpost to something else. He has made the mistake of allowing himself to think that he is an end in himself. This is the sort of thing that happens when you hear people making speeches about themselves, rather than about the person they're supposed to be introducing, or retired film stars who are suddenly given a chance to be centre stage after ten years in which no one has heard a thing about them; they revel in it rather pathetically.

Well, Jesus was under no such misapprehension. Throughout John's gospel he's pointing to his Father. He well understands that the true purpose of his presence is to reveal the Father. Like all human beings, he is constituted by his relation to what is other than himself. In his case, the other is not the social other, the world, with its distortions and violence mixed in with its love and goodness, but the completely transcendent other, the gratuitous other, the Father, whose gratuitous love for him Jesus knows.

Throughout John's gospel, Jesus underlines his dependence on the Father, that without him he can do nothing, that he does what he sees his Father do. He is a completely other-related person. Moved by another. It was perhaps this that disconcerted his contemporaries, and led them to suspect that he might be possessed by a demon. It was clear to them that he was moved by another. This, I might indicate as an aside, was exactly the impact caused on a friend of mine by a recent series of conversations with Mother Teresa: he came away most struck by the evident way in which she is moved by another.

The point of these remarks is that Jesus' real concern is that people should know the Father, not him. At the same time he is aware that he is revealing the Father, and that it is only through him that a real knowledge of the Father is made available. That is: it is only in seeing the pattern of Jesus' life, lived with the intelligence of the victim, that it becomes possible to know the Father, who is revealed only in the casting out. Let me try to make that clearer. The whole process of Jesus' life, leading up to and including his death, is what defines who the Father is. This is because the life is lived in obedient response to the Father's love, and is an exact imitation of the Father's love lived out in the conditions of the human race. The imitation reveals the one imitated. It was Jesus' life and death that made possible the human discovery of who the Father really is.

So, Jesus makes himself known, not as an end in himself, but strictly as the means of revealing the Father. His famous response to Philip in John 14 says exactly this: 'I am the way, the truth and the life; no one comes to the Father but by me.' What Jesus is, he is as revealing the Father. Later on, this is made clearer still when Jesus says, 'and this is eternal life, that they know thee the only true God, and Jesus Christ whom thou has sent'. (John 17.3). The last words of Jesus' last discourse before the trial and crucifixion are as follows: 'O righteous Father, the world has not known thee, but I have known thee; and these know that thou hast sent me. I made known to them thy name, and I will make it

known, that the love with which thou hast loved me
may be in them, and I in them' (John 17.25-6).

Jesus' interest then, is that we know the Father, for
that is what is really going to do us good. Now we can
work out what he considers to be knowing the Father
from what he says explicitly about *not* knowing the
Father. Listen to this: 'If the world hates you, know
that it has hated me before it hated you. If you were of
the world, the world would love its own, but because
you are not of the world, but I chose you out of the
world, therefore the world hates you. Remember the
word that I said to you, "a servant is not greater than
his master." If they persecuted me, they will persecute
you; if they kept my word, they will keep yours also.
But all this they will do on my account, because they do
not know him who sent me.' Here it could not be made
clearer that not knowing the Father, and being involved
in persecuting, are the same thing. Should this need to
be developed further, a few verses on, still in chapter
16, we find this: 'They will put you out of the
synagogues; indeed, the hour is coming when whoever
kills you will think he is offering service to God. And
they will do this because they have not known the
Father, nor me.' Once again, not knowing the Father is
the same thing as being involved in casting out, and in
persecuting, even when this is apparently done in the
service of God. Knowing the Father is the same as the
intelligence of the victim.

Now, this is not a surprise which Jesus springs on his
disciples suddenly, just before his crucifixion. Chapter
8 of John's gospel contains an extraordinary discussion
of Jesus with some Pharisees about knowing the Father.
The Pharisees challenge Jesus about whether or not he
is bearing witness to himself, and Jesus replies that his
Father bears witness to him also. Then he indicates to
the Pharisees, 'You know neither me nor my Father - if
you knew me, you would know my Father also.' The
dialogue continues, with Jesus introducing a radical

criterion in his discussion of the Father. The Pharisees are descendants of Abraham, but they do not know the Father. And this is shown by their attempt to kill Jesus. The attempt to kill means that the god of whom they are really the sons is the devil, who was a murderer from the beginning. There can be no ecumenical discussion between the God whom they claim is their Father, and the god whose followers are blind to what they do when they cast out and kill; there can be no ecumenical discussion between that god, and the Father whom Jesus knows, who is the one who has sent him, and who is revealed precisely through Jesus' self-giving even as far as being killed. These are quite irreconcilable principles. So, when Jesus says, 'you have not known him' (8.55), once again, the definition of not knowing the Father is being involved in casting out and lynching: 'So they took up stones to throw at him'. The definition of knowing the Father is, once again, the intelligence of the victim.

Knowing the Father means becoming aware of how God actually does relate to the world: by loving it, and sending his Son to it to be the expiation of our sins. It means therefore, that there is no knowledge of Jesus without an awareness of Jesus as having been sent in the intelligence of the victim - giving himself freely so as to enable us to be set free from our patterns of relating based on violence. And this is a very disturbing thing. It is the sort of knowledge that can only be practical. There is no knowledge of the Father, or of Jesus, that is not also a practical intelligence regarding how we relate to those who are cast out. There is no knowledge of the Father that can be acquired in isolation from the development of our practical relations with the constant hidden and not so hidden lynchings in our world. To give a small example: the Protestant villagers in Vichy France who hid 5,000 Jews right under the noses of their oppressors for the duration of the war knew the Father; by contrast the German theologians who were happy to rewrite theology so as to make Jesus a sort of Aryan, and who either ignored, or turned a blind eye to the persecution of the Jews; however great their devotion, their prayer life, their zeal, the number of doctorates they wielded, they did not know the Father, and there's an end to it.

Knowing Jesus, therefore, is a part, a necessary part, of knowing the Father. The two point to each other. The Father wants us to see himself in Jesus so that we may start to build a new humanity from the victim, rather than over against victims as we continually do. Jesus reveals the Father by his obedient imitation, even to the point of death, so that all our fantasies about God are destroyed for ever, and the image of God is recast as that which is subversive of all our identities, and unities, and groups, and certainties. What links the Father and Jesus, therefore, is the intelligence of the victim. It is in the light of the intelligence of the victim that we can begin to understand the relationship between the two - the love for us that involved sending Jesus, the love for Jesus that involved sending, and raising him up, the love which Jesus had for his Father which involved giving himself for us knowingly to victimization. It is this knowledge of the intelligence of the victim which sets us free: the truth which sets us free is the truth of the victim. The Counsellor, the Spirit of truth, who is the advocate for the defence against the lynching of the world, this is the intelligence of the victim, bearing witness to the truth which flows from the victim. It is for this reason that Jesus told his disciples in Luke 12.11, 'And when they bring you before the authorities, do not be anxious how or what you are to answer, or what you are to say; for the Holy Spirit will teach you in that very hour what you ought to say.' And no wonder that the Holy Spirit will do just that; it will not be a sort of additional function of the Holy Spirit to do that as well as all sorts of other things. As I hope has become clear by now, the Holy Spirit *is* the intelligence of the victim.

You may remember that at the beginning of this book, I quoted from the preacher to the pontifical household:

> But what is the primary aim of all evangelization and of all catechesis? Possibly that of teaching people a certain number of eternal truths, or of passing on Christian values to the rising generation? No, it is to bring people to a personal encounter with Jesus Christ, the only Saviour by making them his 'disciples'.

Well, I hope that now, at the end of this book, this last affirmation is more meaningful. Cast your mind back to John chapter 8, and the discussion with the Pharisees. Jesus challenges the absolute certainty which the Pharisees had that they knew God because they knew Abraham, and were his children. He challenges it by redefining 'Father' in such a way that no amount of heredity, no amount of group-belonging, no amount of culture could make available. The Father is known only in the casting out of the Son.

That means that for each of us, knowing Jesus, and through him, knowing the Father, cannot be simply something learnt. It must be something discovered, as the intelligence of the victim makes fresh in our lives the possibilities of relating anew to those towards whom we are blind, to those whom we exclude. It is this discovery, gradual as it may be, fed by the making present of the victim risen as forgiveness in the life of the Church and the sacraments, involving a constantly critical reappraisal of our ways of belonging, our repetitive patterns of relating, which is what the papal preacher referred to as our 'personal encounter' with Jesus Christ. As our eyes are gradually opened, and we become disciples by serving those whom the intelligence of the victim reveals to us, so we will find that we have come to know Jesus, and the Father. We will be surprised to discover that what appears to be a road leading only to exclusion, and narrowing horizons, turns instead into a highway of ever increasing diversity, and the richness of learning to be moved by Another, Another who is quite without rivalry or possessiveness. And there we will know without the hidden traps of our self-delusion blinding us; we will know as we are known, and discover that our knowledge of Jesus was nothing at all compared to his knowledge of, and love for, us. But that would be another book.

Questions

1. How does knowledge of Jesus enable you to relax into being loved as one of the 'crude mass of humanity'? Do you find that you need to insist on imagining goodies and baddies among those who surround you in order for your faith to make sense?

2. How do you understand repentance? Is any repentance really possible before you have had your heart widened by the discovery that you are loved?

3. How do we learn to imitate the self-giving victim? What is meant by the claim that this is a new sort of practical learning?

4. What is wrong with any claim to knowing Jesus that doesn't have public practical consequences? What does this mean in terms of learning to stand up for those who are being cast out, especially by those who think that in doing so, they are serving God?

5. What sense does it make to claim that we

know the Father apart from our learning of a new fraternity with Jesus and those who are being cast out? How does our learning of fraternity with Jesus destroy our fantasies and projections about God? Is there a knowledge of God that is not profoundly, yet serenely, subversive of our identities and ways of relating to each other?

6. If someone now asks you whether you know Jesus, how would you reply? How would you have replied before reading this book? Has your answer changed? Why?

Further Reading

If you have enjoyed, or profited from, the approach adopted in this book, you might like to know of other works in which a similar understanding is at work:

James Alison, *Living in the End Times: The Last Things Reimagined*. London: SPCK, 1996
  The Joy of Being Wrong: Original Sin through Easter Eyes. New York: Crossroad, 1998
Gil Bailie, *Violence Unveiled: Humanity at the Crossroad*. New York: Crossroad, 1995
René Girard, *Violence and the Sacred*. Baltimore and London: Johns Hopkins University Press, 1977
  Things Hidden Since the Foundation of the World. London: Athlone Press, 1987
  The Scapegoat. London: Athlone Press, 1986
  Resurrection from the Underground: Fyodor Dostoevsky. New York: Crossroad, 1997
Robert Hamerton-Kelly, *Sacred Violence: Paul's Hermeneutic of the Cross*. Minneapolis: Fortress Press, 1992
Raymund Schwager SJ, *Must There be Scapegoats? Violence and Redemption in the Bible*. San Francisco: Harper and Row, 1987
  Jesus of Nazareth: How He Understood His Life. New York: Crossroad, 1998
James Williams, *The Bible, Violence and the Sacred: Liberation from the Myth of Sanctioned Violence*. San Francisco: Harper and Row, 1991

Index

Biblical references are given under the book in question, and appear in brackets after the page number: e.g. Hosea (book of prophet) 38 (6.1-2)

Printed in the USA
CPSIA information can be obtained
at www.ICGtesting.com
LVHW010103090823
754721LV00003B/310

9 780281 065035